THE CANAL & RIVER SECTIONS
OF THE
AIRE AND CALDER NAVIGATION

Inextricably linked with the Aire & Calder Navigation was the Compartment Boat (Tom Pudding) operation whereby up to forty tons of coal were loaded at various West Riding colliery staithes into each 20ft x 15ft iron 'pan' having a depth of 9ft. These were then assembled into trains to be towed by steam tugs to Goole where they were tipped in turn by one of several distinctive hydraulically-powered hoists on the dock estate into sea-going vessels for delivery to near-European ports or English south- and east-coast ports , including the River Thames. The system, devised by W H Bartholomew as a response to encroaching railway services, began in the 1860s and continued for over one and a quarter centuries. Originally, the pans were push-towed in steerable trains of up to twelve units but were pull-towed from about 1900. During their lifetime, 55 million tons were carried by the puddings, usually in nineteen-pan trains which, throughout the twentieth century, could pass unbroken through Bulholme lock and those below. It was difficult to find return cargoes to bring back up the navigation from Goole, especially after the First World War, though wool, wire and oil seeds were carried at various times. The system's best year was 1913 when 1,560,000 tons of coal were brought to Goole using 18 steam tugs and 1,010 pans; an average of 7 trains being tipped at Goole on each working day. In 1932, regular cargoes began to be collected from Hatfield colliery on the Sheffield & South Yorkshire Navigation (S&SYN). During the late nineteenth century, Bartholomew had access to Denaby Colliery in mind and this was the motive for construction of the New Junction Canal, opened in 1905, but he had to settle posthumously for having this waterway used to reach Hatfield instead. Bartholomew was also instrumental in persuading the S&SYNC to make several changes to their 'track' in order to facilitate puddings passing up to Denaby (see Wharncliffe Publishing's *Aspects of Doncaster 2*). During the late 1950s, diesel tugs replaced the steam tugs, the demand for coal fell in the 1960s as natural gas gradually replaced coal gas as a domestic and industrial fuel and smokeless fuel loaded at Doncaster and Castleford began to be carried in 1967, completely replacing coal by the early 1970s. The final cargo was carried by the puddings in April 1986.

A 48ft x 15ft steam tug is shown in the 1950s hauling a train of coal-laden puddings through Knottingley, bound for Goole. The photograph was taken looking west from Jackson's Bridge and allows the function of the 'jebus'/false bows/headpiece to be appreciated in preventing the tug's wash building up against the leading pan by lifting that pan to deflect the water beneath and to either side of the train, thus giving a smoother and more efficient pull. *D Wells*

THE CANAL &
RIVER SECTIONS
of the
AIRE & CALDER
NAVIGATION

Mike Taylor

Series Editor
Brian Elliott

Wharncliffe Books

First Published in 2003 by
Wharncliffe Books
an imprint of
Pen and Sword Books Limited,
47 Church Street, Barnsley,
South Yorkshire. S70 2AS

Copyright © Mike Taylor 2003

For up-to-date information on other titles produced under the
Wharncliffe imprint, please telephone or write to:

> **Wharncliffe Books**
> **FREEPOST**
> **47 Church Street**
> **Barnsley**
> **South Yorkshire S70 2BR**
> **Telephone (24 hours): 01226 - 734555**

ISBN: 1-903425-37-9

A CIP catalogue record of this book is available from the
British Library

Front cover illustration: *A Cawoods Hargreaves push tow passing through Knottingley Cutting, loaded with*
coal for Ferrybridge 'C' power station. Norman Burnitt
Back cover illustration: *Discharging wood pulp from the Baltic at Barnsley Paper Mills, 1912.* HKSPS

Printed in the United Kingdom by
CPI UK

CONTENTS

A loaded Tom Pudding train en route for Goole approaches Rawcliffe Bridge.

Aire and Calder Navigation

Owners of the Port of Goole. - Yorkshire's Waterway to the Sea.

For all information apply:—
Head Office,
> AIRE & CALDER
> NAVIGATION,
>> DOCK STREET,
>> LEEDS, 1.

Telephones : 20957-8 ; 30351-3.
Telegrams : NAVIGATION, Leeds.

Dock Office,
> GOOLE—
> STANHOPE STREET.

Telephone : 311-2.
Telegrams : NAVIGATION, Goole.

Dock Office,
> HULL—
> NELSON STREET.

Telephone : 15555-6.
Telegrams : NAVIGATION, Hull.

———

Comprehensive Brochure
sent on request.

A most up-to-date and efficient inland waterway connecting at Leeds with the Leeds & Liverpool Canal.

Direct water communication between the industrial towns of the West Riding of Yorkshire and the Ports on the Rivers Ouse and Humber.

The Navigation possess a large fleet of boats for the carriage of general merchandise, and the waterway is extensively used by Canal Carriers and Traders owning their own craft.

Vessels capable of carrying 150/200 tons can be navigated on the main lines of the waterway.

A large number of Collieries use the waterway for the conveyance of coal by means of the compartment boat system, which is the most efficient and economic method of transport in this country. The Navigation own 1,100 of these compartment boats, which have an aggregate carrying capacity of approximately 40,000 tons.

The total tonnage of traffic passing over the waterway in 1935 was approximately 2½ millions.

The Navigation are extensive land-owners and have ideal sites available for factories and depots.

THE PORT OF GOOLE is the most inland port on the North East Coast of England, and is second to none in its water, rail and road facilities. The Port is equipped with up-to-date electric and hydraulic hoists, cranes, and anti coal-breakage appliances.

There are nine wet docks with a water area of 46½ acres and three miles of quayage. Extensive shed and warehouse accommodation is available in addition to large and spacious wharves.

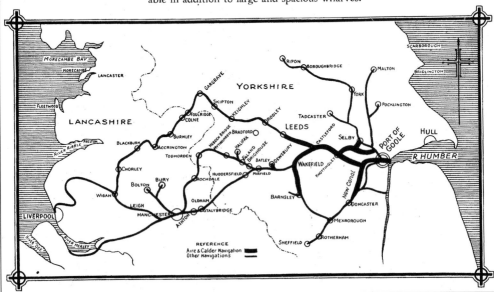

This advertisement for the Aire & Calder Navigation dates from the mid-1930s.
Waterways Museum, Goole

INTRODUCTION

By the early eighteenth century and over fifty years before England's so-called 'canal mania', the Undertakers of the Aire & Calder Navigation or, as they are referred to in this book, the Aire & Calder Navigation Company (A&CNC), prompted by the wool and cloth merchants of Leeds and Wakefield, had adapted the Yorkshire rivers Aire and Calder under an *Act of Parliament* of 1699 to become Britain's premier inland waterway. After a merely satisfactory first sixty years which saw little reinvestment in the navigation, exemplary management and constant improvements characterised the A&CN during the following two centuries of private ownership and continued after nationalisation in 1948. A general chronology is given below with historical details of specific local sites, some carrying companies and craft in use contained within relevant captions in the pictorial section of the book:

pre-1400 Tidal River Aire navigable by cargo boats up to Knottingley at favourable states of the tide. Woollen goods for export delivered here by packhorse to be transhipped to craft.

1462: York Corporation made responsible for keeping a navigable channel of the Aire up to Knottingley's King's Mill, free from obstructions.

1700: A&CNC completed short canal cuts and nine 60ft x 15ft locks with masonry walls and timber flooring on River Aire to permit 15-ton capacity boats to reach Leeds from Knottingley on a 3ft draught.

1701: A&CNC completed short canal cuts and four locks, similar to those up to Leeds, on River Calder to permit 15-ton capacity boats to reach Wakefield from Knottingley.

1702: Act of 1699 made A&CNC responsible for Aire to Weeland, 8½ miles below Knottingley. Locks and weirs completed on this stretch at Beal and Haddlesey.
Transhipment between sea-going and inland waterway craft developed at Rawcliffe and Airmyn.

1758: Regular shipping service to London of goods transhipped at Airmyn began.

1770: Calder & Hebble Navigation (C&HN) completed (Wakefield to Sowerby Bridge).

1774: *Act of Parliament* passed containing proposals made by John Smeaton (1724-92) for improvement of A&CN, including Selby Canal, various other new cuts and extension of A&CNC's responsibility for lower Aire from Weeland to confluence with River Ouse below Airmyn.

1775: Knostrop Cut and Castleford Cut constructed with flood locks at their upper ends to allow traffic to move when the rivers were in flood. A&CNC began to buy up riverside mills which hitherto had become a nuisance to them by lowering water levels thereby grounding craft.

1778: Selby Canal opened, designed by William Jessop (1745-1814), Smeaton's assistant, allowing craft passing between A&CN and River Ouse to avoid shallows on River Aire below Haddlesey.

1785: Locks now rebuilt and waterways dredged to accept 45-ton craft, as recommended by Smeaton.

1799: Barnsley Canal opened to Barnsley (to Barnby Bridge in 1802).

1802: A&CNC's Lake Lock maintenance, repair and boatbuilding yard opened.

1804: Dearne & Dove Canal opened.
Cross-Pennine Rochdale Canal opened.

1811: Cross-Pennine Huddersfield Narrow Canal completed.

1816: Cross-Pennine Leeds & Liverpool Canal (L&LC) opened.

1818: New basin opened near Leeds Bridge, called Leeds Terminus.

1826: Knottingley & Goole Canal (actually Ferrybridge-Goole) and the Port of Goole opened, authorised by 1820 *Act of Parliament.*

1831: Steam tug service introduced for A&CNC's own flyboats (craft running to a timetable).

1835: Improvements to Leeds branch and River Aire above Ferrybridge completed, waterway now 7ft deep with locks 18ft wide.

1839: Improvements to Wakefield branch (Calder Cut) completed, including Stanley Ferry aqueduct.

1843: New Dock/Clarence Dock/Tatie Basin opened at Leeds.

1845: Arches lock branch of Leeds & Liverpool Canal completed leading to River Aire above the weir.

1848: Railways (Lancashire & Yorkshire and Manchester & Leeds) entered Goole Docks.

1851: A&CNC headquarters transferred from Wakefield to Leeds.

1853: Thomas Hammond Bartholomew (A&CN Engineer) died and was succeeded by his son William Hammond Bartholomew.

1857: Steam tugs introduced to tow by-traders' boats between Goole and Wakefield and Goole and Leeds.

1865: Between 1850 and 1880, nearly 200 new collieries were opened in the West Riding.
Compartment boats (Tom Puddings) introduced to deliver West Riding coal to Goole for export.

1867: Stone-arched bridges over waterway replaced by girder bridges to increase both headroom and width of canal.
Lengthening of locks between Goole and Castleford to 206ft completed.

1869: Lock lengthening to 206ft from Castleford to Wakefield completed.

1873: Lock lengthening to 206ft from Castleford to Leeds completed.
Lake Lock yard replaced by Stanley Ferry yard as A&CNC's principal repair yard.

1874: Wooden jetty built on Lower Ouse at Blacktoft.

1875: W H Bartholomew became General Manager of A&CNC as well as Engineer. A&CNC purchased Barnsley Canal, having leased it since 1854. They enlarged locks to 84ft x 15ft.

1878: Dewsbury old cut purchased. 1774-built Bradford Canal (off the L&LC) purchased jointly by A&CNC and L&LCC.

1881: Goole repair yard opened by A&CNC.

1884: A&CNC became responsible for River Ouse just below Hook railway bridge to Trent Falls and began building training walls, eventually completed in 1935.

1885: Southfield reservoirs opened giving better supply of water to eastern end of A&CN and Goole docks.

1900: More lock improvements made between Goole and Castleford. Barges of 200 tons capacity able to reach Leeds, 120 tons to Wakefield.

1905: New Junction Canal opened linking A&CN with S&SYN, having one 215ft x 22ft x 9½ft lock.
River Aire at Hunslet rerouted to pass north of Knostrop Cut.

1919: W H Bartholomew died.

1922: Whitley and Pollington locks enlarged to 460ft x 22ft, able to accept a 19-unit Tom Pudding train or general merchandise tug and 8 barges without splitting plus other conventional craft in embayments (Bulholme Lock had been enlarged to these dimensions in 1901).
Bradford Canal closed.

1944: Huddersfield Narrow Canal abandoned.

1946: Breach on Barnsley Canal leading to closure in 1953.

1948: Nationalisation of A&CN, becoming part of British Transport Commission's Docks & Inland Waterways Executive (D&IWE).

1952: Rochdale Canal abandoned.

1953: Port of Goole separated from former A&CN as D&IWE broken up. Port and lower Ouse now part of British Transport Docks Board (BTDB), former A&CN west of Goole part of British Transport Waterways (BTW).

1956: Blacktoft jetty rebuilt in concrete.

1958: New depot and warehouse opened at Knostrop, near Leeds.
New diesel-powered Tom Pudding tugs built over next two years.

1963: British Waterways Board (BW) took over former A&CN west of Goole and are still responsible for it in 2003.

1966: Large compartment boats powered by push-tugs introduced by a private company to supply Ferrybridge 'C' power station with coal. (traffic ended 2002)

1967: Large petrol contract (Immingham to Leeds) signed, Goole-Leeds length enlarged to take 500-ton capacity craft. Locks mechanised and Thwaite island removed to allow traffic to start in following year.

1978: Enlargement of canal between Goole and Leeds and modification of locks to take 700-tonne tankers.

1981: Associated British Ports (ABP) succeeded BTDB in controlling Goole docks, lower Ouse, Humber and Hull docks.
New aqueduct completed at Stanley Ferry.

1986: Tom Puddings finished.

1987: BW sold off its waterside depots, including Knostrop, and disposed of its commercial vessels, thus ending a 200-year-old tradition of the navigation owners carrying in their own craft on the A&CN.

1988: River Aire flooded adjacent opencast coal workings near Castleford.

1995: As a consequence of 1988 flooding, new line of canal and new Lemonroyd lock opened, Kippax lock eliminated.

This book concentrates on the carriage of cargoes by inland waterway craft, though shipping is mentioned when this is relevant. Some early twentieth century annual tonnages illustrate the extent of traffic on the A&CN:

1898: 2,391,722	1918: 1,594,441	1938: 2,399,696
1903: 2,514,789	1923: 2,864,174	1943: 1,771,027
1908: 3,082,595	1928: 2,489,094	
1913: 3,597,921	1933: 2,064,791	

As expected, troughs appear during the First World War (1914-18), the depression years of the late 1920s and early 1930s, and the Second World War (1939-45). There was a decline in coal traffic in the 1960s and 1970s caused by the countrywide changeover from coal gas to natural gas as a domestic and industrial fuel. A decline in general cargo also occurred at about the same time as the capacities of railway wagons and lorries steadily increased, making their usage more economic. These, and other factors including 'blacking' by Hull dockers, led to several canal carriers ceasing to trade in the 1970s. Annual tonnages fell from over 3 million in the early 1960s to 2 million by the 1970s but then gradually rose again to over $2\frac{1}{2}$ million by the mid-1970s, four fifths of which was accounted for by coal deliveries to Ferrybridge power stations. The recent loss of this traffic will produce a marked decrease in 2003.

Representative illustrations of the craft of major carriers on the waterway during the twentieth century have been included. Almost all vessels had facilities for their crews to 'live aboard' with the standards of accommodation provided steadily rising over the years from spartan to almost luxurious.

Chapters in the book are based on strip maps or 'sectional plans' provided by the Waterways Museum at Goole. These were published in the 1930s when the waterway was enjoying a prosperous period and show sufficient pre-1930s detail to look backwards as well as enabling post-1930s changes to be visualised. They are not drawn to a constant scale but more accurate distances may be estimated by reference to the topographical map following this introduction. The text alongside each strip map is based on 1930s descriptions, standard historical accounts, information from various published 'guides' and my own observations. The illustrations are in random chronological order and arranged in strip map order, working from top to bottom of the corresponding page.

Perversely, the book proper begins off the A&CN to include the L&LC and part of the River Aire above Leeds Bridge. Otherwise the destinations of traffic passing through Leeds, ninety per cent of which was coal, would be omitted, giving an incomplete picture of the city's waterway activity. It is also convenient to include the Bradford Canal in this first section.

Apart from a few etchings, the illustrations date from the twentieth century and have been selected from my own photographs and collection of postcards, which are uncredited, and various other sources which are acknowledged individually.

Mike Taylor, July 2003

ACKNOWLEDGEMENTS

I am grateful for the information and general help with the preparation of this book provided by the late Stan Barrass, Douglas Carey, Ron and Sheila Gosney, Loveday Herridge, Jack Hall, Brian Masterman and Jarvis Whitton

I have received considerable assistance with provision of illustrations from the Waterways Museum, Goole and the book would be poorer without the photographs of Norman Burnitt and Jarvis Whitton. Help in acquiring illustrations has also kindly been given by Mike Brown, Ron Gosney, Hargreaves, Harkers, Andy Horn, Alan West and John H Whitaker Ltd.

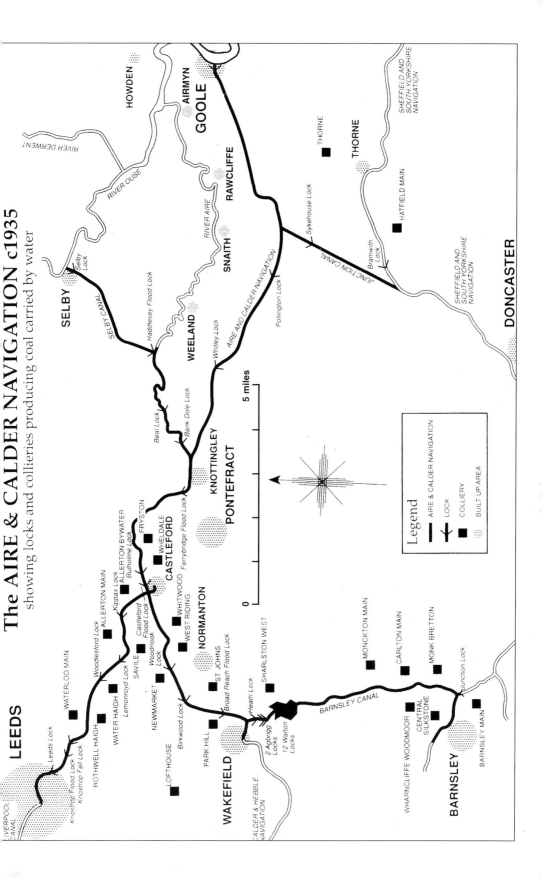

The AIRE & CALDER NAVIGATION c1935
showing locks and collieries producing coal carried by water

LEEDS

Legend
- AIRE & CALDER NAVIGATION
- LOCK
- COLLIERY
- BUILT-UP AREA

SELBY

HOWDEN

AIRMYN

GOOLE

RIVER DERWENT

RIVER OUSE

RAWCLIFFE

THORNE

THORNE

RIVER AIRE

SNAITH

WEELAND

HATFIELD MAIN

Selby Lock

SELBY CANAL

Haddlesey Flood Lock

Whitley Lock

Pollington Lock

AIRE AND CALDER NAVIGATION

Sykehouse Lock

Bramwith Lock

JUNCTION CANAL

SHEFFIELD AND SOUTH YORKSHIRE NAVIGATION

SHEFFIELD AND SOUTH YORKSHIRE NAVIGATION

DONCASTER

Beal Lock

Bank Dole Lock

KNOTTINGLEY

PONTEFRACT

5 miles

0

FRYSTON

WHELDALE

CASTLEFORD

Ferrybridge Flood Lock

Castleford Flood Lock

Bulholme Lock

Kippax Lock

ALLERTON BYWATER

ALLERTON MAIN

Woodlesford Lock

WATERLOO MAIN

WATER HAIGH

Lemonoyd Lock

ROTHWELL HAIGH

Knostrop Fall Lock

Knostrop Flood Lock

Leeds Lock

LIVERPOOL CANAL

SAVILE

Woodnook Lock

NEWMARKET

LOFTHOUSE

Birkwood Lock

PARK HILL

ST JOHNS

Broad Reach Flood Lock

Heath Lock

SHARLSTON WEST

WHITWOOD

WEST RIDING

NORMANTON

WAKEFIELD

CALDER & HEBBLE NAVIGATION

2 Agbrigg Locks

12 Walton Locks

Barnsley Canal

MONCKTON MAIN

CARLTON MAIN

MONK BRETTON

WHARNCLIFFE WOODMOOR

CENTRAL SILKSTONE

Junction Lock

BARNSLEY MAIN

BARNSLEY

CHAPTER ONE

Above Leeds to Castleford

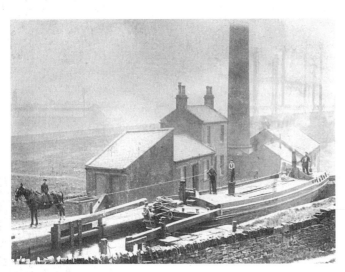

The 3½-mile, 10-lock Bradford Canal which joined the Leeds & Liverpool Canal at Shipley was opened in 1774, closed as a health hazard in 1867 and reopened in 1873 before being purchased jointly by the A&CNC and L&LCC in 1878. Here, c.1900, the Pearson family's horse-drawn *Harry*, with Tom at the helm and his son standing on the lutchet (central towing mast), is preparing to leave the lower lock of the Spinkhill staircase pair for the upper lock. The vessel would then pen up this prior to travelling half a mile along the summit level to the canal's terminal basin. *Jim Beckett Collection*

The L&L shortboat *Victoria* is moored above the Bradford Canal's Stone Bridge c.1900, after loading stone setts at the adjacent wharf. *Waterways Museum, Goole.*

The Bradford Canal was closed finally in 1922 but, until the early 1930s, coal was barged a quarter-mile up the waterway into the remaining chamber of Windhill lock, the closest to the L&LC's main line. Here it was discharged by an electrically powered hoist, via a hopper, into either horse-hauled wagons owned by a nearby dye house or a local coal merchant's lorries. A coal-laden L&L shortboat working on this traffic is shown c.1930 below the lock. *Frank Woodall*

The L&LC above Leeds was used extensively to supply coal collected from collieries alongside the A&CN to West Yorkshire's Pennine towns such as Skipton. Here, prior to ascending Bingley Five-rise locks, one of the most spectacular sites on Britain's inland waterways, Thorntons' dumb 60ft x 14ft *Edith*, is moored with one of that coal merchant's steam towing barges in attendance.

Kirkstall Brewery Bridge
Canal Wharf & Warehouse (J. W. King)

Wither Bridge

Redcote Bridge

Redcote Branch Canal
Leeds Corporation Electricity Works

L.M.S. Railway Bridge

Armley Mill Bridge

Canal Road Bridge
A. E. De Barr Ltd., Carriers and Coal
Merchants
L.N.E. Railway Bridge

Albion Works (Greenwood & Batley Ltd.)

J. Hattersley, Spindle Works
Canal Mills (Maurice Dixon)
Castletown Mill (Thos. Luety & Co. Ltd.)

Springs Garden Lock

Oddy Locks, 2-Rise
Wellington Road Bridge
St. Ann's Ing Lock
L.M.S. & L.N.E. Railway Bridges
Monk Bridge
L.M.S. Railway Bridge

Monk Bridge Iron & Steel Co. Ltd.

J. Wyatt Ltd., Refiners
F. Sunley, Coal Factor
Wharf, etc. (Canal Transport Ltd)
3-ton Crane
Arches Lock, leading to Leeds Corporation
Whitehall Electricity Works, and
Joseph Watson & Sons, Soap Manufac-
turers.

Globe Road Works (Lewis & Co.)
Tower Works (Harding & Rhodes Ltd.)
Canal Wharves
David Speight & Son, Building Con-
tractors
Office Lock
Canal Lock House & Office

W. E. Hickman Ltd.
T. B. Morley & Co., Plumbers' Mer-
chants
W. Rider & Co., Boat Yard
C. P. Murray & Co., Builders' Merchants
Silkburn Coal Company Ltd.
B. Spink, Haulage Contractor
A. Blakebrough & Co., Drysalters
L.M.S. & L.N.E. Stations

Dalton & Higgins, Stone Merchants
Canal Wharves & Warehouses (Canal
Transport Ltd.)
Depot for Tate & Lyle Ltd., Sugar
Depot for Fairrie & Co., Sugar
River Lock
Leeds Terminus
River Aire (Junction with Aire & Calder
Navigation for East Yorkshire and the
East Coast).

RIVER AIRE

This map of the Leeds & Liverpool Canal between Leeds and Kirkstall, dates from the mid-1930s and shows the access route to/from wharves on the Aire via Arches lock.
Waterways Museum, Goole

Leeds Corporation Electricity Department (LCED) opened
Kirkstall power station in 1931. A loop had been constructed
off the L&LC to accommodate craft delivering coal and
LCED's steel motor barge *Arc*, built by Dunstons of Thorne, is
shown near the discharge apparatus on the 'Redcote Branch
Canal'. The traffic ended in 1965. *Richard Dunston*

The LCED's *Spark* heads up the L&LC towards
Kirkstall power station in the 1950s with a load of
coal and towing another vessel. *Yorkshire Evening Press*

Arthur, owned by Holdens of Skipton and renamed from *Mersey* after its purchase from L&LC's Canal Transport, is shown passing the arm to Arches lock whilst carrying coal from Parkhill to Skipton gasworks in the 1950s. Powered by a one-cylinder 21hp Widdop engine, the helmsman had no shelter from the elements on deck. The gasworks closed in 1961. *Jack Hall*

LCED's dumb barge *No 27 Light* is launched into the Aire from William Rider & Company's boatyard, visible on the previous photograph, which existed above the L&LC's River lock from 1863 to 1972. Wooden vessels were built at the yard until the 1950s and thererafter it concentrated on the maintenance of existing craft. *H Hudson Collection*

There were two extensive users of the A&CN situated alongside the north bank of the River Aire above Leeds: Watsons' soapworks and Whitehall power station. Both premises were accessible to 'soaphouse' size (63½ft x 14½ft) craft via the L&LC, the 1840s-built Arches lock and a crossing of the river made using a line taken up to a pole 150 yards above the lock before shearing across. This advertising card, dated 1945, shows the soap works which received vegetable oils and boxwood by water.

A light coal barge is shown emerging from the L&LC's River lock, with its adjacent canal warehouses, into the Aire. The river at this point was described by Tom Bradley in 1893 within the *Yorkshire Weekly Post:*

> *In a lazy sluggish fashion it drags its course through the town, a putrid bed of filthy excrement where thousands of people daily pass and are obliged to breathe its fever laden vapours.* T Young

In the late 1960s, when this photograph was taken, Leeds Industrial Cooperative Society (LICS) were retailers of domestic coal barged to their Victoria wharf depot on the River Aire, just upstream of and on the opposite bank to the L&LC's River lock. They had closed their other depot near Leeds locks in 1964.

LICS began collecting coal by water from A&CN collieries for delivery to Leeds in 1880 using their large fleet of horse-hauled dumb boats. The wooden ones were built and maintained at Riders' yard nearby, the steel vessels were built by Dunstons of Thorne. The Society hired a steam tug in 1918 and purchased their own, *Unity*, in 1921 and, *Albion*, in 1936, both built by Scarrs' of Hessle. The once-extensive traffic ended in 1975. *P L Smith*

LICS's 60ft x 14ft towing barge *Albion* and diesel tug *The President* are moored at Victoria Wharf in the 1960s. *Michael Streat*

Built for LICS, the 45ft x 12ft *Bernard C Wallace* to be powered by a 50hp engine lies ready for launching and, shortly after entering the water, (inset) at Richard Dunston's Thorne yard in 1958. The vessel was subsequently renamed *The President* and sold in 1971. *Norman Burnitt*

Leeds City Tramways' permanent way yard was opened in October 1914 on the north bank of the River Aire between Victoria Bridge and Leeds Bridge. Almost immediately, it was requisitioned for the war effort and not returned until September 1919. This picture of a vessel delivering salt for winter treatment of the city's tramlines was taken shortly afterwards. Leeds Tramways also used the A&CN to bring coal to their 1897-built power station situated on the north bank of the Aire above Crown Point Bridge in the early twentieth century.

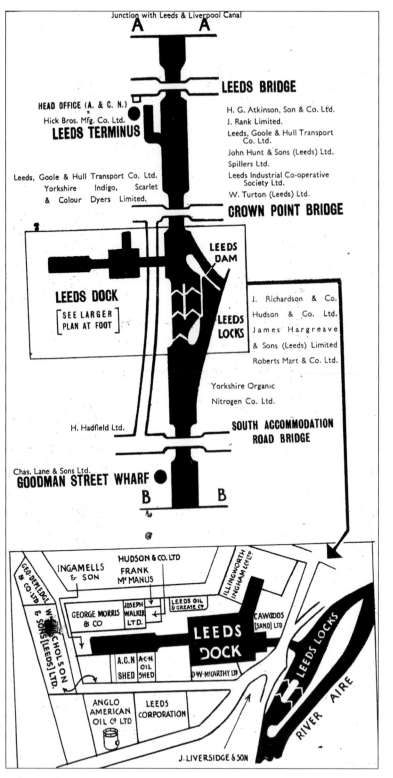

The A&CNC moved their head offices from Wakefield to Leeds in 1851, having constructed a new dock off the river (Leeds Terminus) below Leeds Bridge in 1818. Shortly after, timber sheds and brick-built warehouses were added here, along with more warehouses across the Aire, at the foot of Warehouse Hill leading up to The Calls. They then moved into new head offices built on this same site in 1906. It was proudly advertised that thirty-seven hydraulic cranes and hoists were available here in the 1930s and that over half a million tons of cargo passed annually through Leeds by water at the time. A declining amount of the non-coal cargo in the 1930s was handled by the A&CNC's once essential General Merchandise Towing Service.

The three-acre Leeds Dock/New Dock/Clarence Dock/Tatie Basin, just above Leeds locks, was built in 1843 to handle coal, timber and aggregate. In addition to cranes capable of handling twenty-ton lifts, it also had warehouses to store vegetable oils and wool. Of the companies named on the map as having wharves on the north bank of the Aire opposite Leeds locks, only Hargreaves were still there when a BTW guide was published in 1960.

This postcard scene was photographed looking downstream towards the old Leeds Bridge over the River Aire, where the A&CN begins, and the company's warehouses beyond. The bridge was demolished in 1871.

The wrought iron replacement Leeds Bridge of 1873 is shown with the former A&CNC steam tug *Emma*, under hire to LICS, towing craft upstream in 1920. There was no tow-path on this stretch of the Aire between Leeds Bridge and the L&LC so two steam tugs ran back and forth all day until the 1940s towing craft between these points. Navigation company warehouses may be seen on each side of the waterway. *D Wells Collection*

In 1906, when the A&CNC moved into these new head offices adjacent to Leeds Bridge, they were responsible for over 80 miles of inland waterway. This comprised 24 miles between Goole and Calder Mouth, Castleford, 10 miles between Calder Mouth and Leeds, 8 miles between Calder Mouth and Wakefield, $14\frac{1}{2}$ miles of the Barnsley Canal, $16\frac{1}{2}$ miles between Knottingley and Selby, $2\frac{1}{2}$ miles of the Bradford Canal, $5\frac{1}{2}$ miles of the New Junction Canal and 1 mile of Dewsbury Old Cut. *A&CNC.*

The evening arrival of the Goole to Leeds tow of both A&CNC and by-traders' craft is pictured here in the 1920s. The service was described as 'the general merchandise tow' to distinguish it from the puddings tows (a similar service ran between Goole and Wakefield) The tug and three barges would have needed two pennings at each of the five locks above Castleford, taking a total of between 12 and 18 hours for the complete voyage. After coaling at the depot, the four-man crew would bed down aboard the tug for a short sleep before setting off back to Goole with a return tow in the early hours of the next day.

River Aire, Leeds.

One of the A&CNC's fleet of Scammell 'mechanical horse' and trailer units is shown at Dock Street Terminus, Leeds, in the mid-1930s loaded with bales of wool for onward delivery from the quayside by road. Road services were originally established between Leeds and Bradford to handle raw wool and cloth after closure of the Bradford Canal in 1922 and quickly became an essential part of the A&CNC's service throughout the West Riding. *A&CNC*

The merchandise tows finished about the time of nationalisation due to a lack of demand for the service as most craft were then self-propelled. Built by Harkers of Knottingley in 1949, after nationalisation as the merchandise tugs were being scrapped, the D&IWE's *Beta B W* was one of the towing barges used to pull the few remaining dumb craft requiring the service and is shown in the 1950s, after lengthening, moored within the covered warehousing space at Leeds Terminus. Additionally, these craft could tow on the Humber, thereby dispensing with the need for a Goole-Hull tow of craft working to/from Hull. *BTW*

John Hunt & Sons were founded in 1860 and delivered many cargoes to the soap works alongside the River Aire above Leeds in their dumb soaphouse size craft. The A&CNC's general merchandise tows were used to move the vessels until 1930 when Hunts had their own towing barges built. The company also transhipped cargoes at Leeds for wharves on the L&LC. Between 1958 and 1966, Hunts had five 250-ton capacity diesel craft built and one of these, the Harker-built *Doris Hunt,* is shown within Leeds Terminus at Dock Street where the company leased warehousing and wharf space until they ceased trading by water in 1974. *Waterways Museum, Goole*

Looking across the river from Leeds Terminus towards Warehouse Hill in the 1940s, transhipment of tobacco brought ex-ship from Hull by Spillers' dumb barge *Ril Florence* is taking place into a L&L shortboat for onward delivery to Liverpool. The procedure was necessary due to the L&LC's inability to accept the large, deep-draughted barge that had reached Leeds via the A&CN. Again the crew's minimal protection from the elements is evident on both craft. A&CNC

Steam keels and dumb craft are moored up to three abreast on the Warehouse Hill side of the Aire with one of the large warehouses and Leeds Bridge visible in the background on this 1920s view looking upriver.

This well-known view into Leeds Dock, dating from the 1930s, is full of detail and tends to be featured in most books on the A&CN. LCED's *No 1* is loaded with fine coal for one of the power stations whilst LICS's *No 12* is carrying large lumps of house coal for their Victoria wharf. Hargreaves' tug *Aire* and some other coal-laden craft are tied up beyond, new puddings are being poled in mid-dock and moored timber barges may also be seen across the water. The dock was often referred to as the 'Tatie Basin' after its earlier use for handling Jersey potatoes imported via Goole and delivered here by A&CNC's flyboats. The Royal Armouries is now established on this site. *A&CNC*

Harkers' tanker barge *Ennerdale H* passes up through Leeds locks to deliver a cargo of petrol to the Esso (formerly Anglo-American) depot in the Tatie Basin in the 1950s. The lock in use was built in the early nineteenth century to the left of the original lock. Harkers were involved with the carriage of petroleum liquids from the 1920s, coming to it from a background of carrying coal tar and other gasworks liquids. They acquired a fleet of tanker barges, most of which were built at their own Knottingley boatyard. *Jarvis Whitton*

LICS's loaded dumb vessels have been towed into Leeds locks (probably by the Society's tug/barge *Albion*) and are being manoeuvred into position by their crews. The lock gates shown were added in the late nineteenth century, effectively forming one large lock where a tug and several dumb barges could be passed through in one penning. LICS were the last users of towed dumb boats on the A&CN. *Yorkshire Evening Press*

Across the Aire from Leeds locks and visible to the left of the previous picture, Hargreaves had a domestic coal depot at East Street wharf and here, in 1955, their 200-ton capacity wooden dumb barges *Hilda* and *Joan* are being discharged by the company's rail-mounted crane. Deliveries by water began in 1906 and the depot closed in 1965. *Hargreaves*

A great initiator of improvements to the A&CN was the 10-year contract between BW, two carriers and Esso to deliver petrol to Leeds. Two of the six 500-ton capacity craft newly-built for the deliveries, Whitakers' *Humber Enterprise* and *Humber Renown* are shown bringing the first cargoes to Leeds in January 1968. The other tankers were Harkers' *Farndale H, Fossdale H* and *Fusedale H* and Cory Tank Lighterage's *Battle Stone*.

BW effectively made a 500-ton capacity waterway between Goole and Leeds out of a 250-ton waterway in little over a year; dredging, deepening locks by chipping away their curved bases and smoothing out bends in the channel. Perhaps to avoid altering and mechanising Leeds locks, BW constructed a 260ft long steel-piled wharf below the locks and an underground pipeline to connect this with Esso's depot in the Tatie Basin. Deliveries here continued until 1982. *Whitakers*

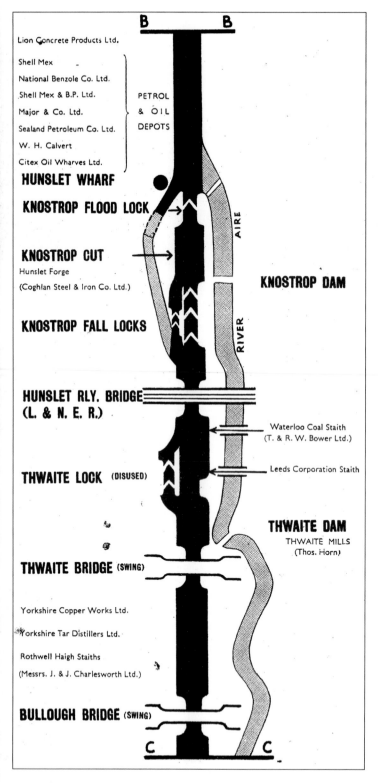

Lion Concrete Products Ltd.

Shell Mex
National Benzole Co. Ltd.
Shell Mex & B.P. Ltd.
Major & Co. Ltd.   PETROL
Sealand Petroleum Co. Ltd.   & OIL
W. H. Calvert   DEPOTS
Citex Oil Wharves Ltd.

HUNSLET WHARF

KNOSTROP FLOOD LOCK

KNOSTROP CUT
Hunslet Forge
(Coghlan Steel & Iron Co. Ltd.)

KNOSTROP FALL LOCKS

AIRE

RIVER

KNOSTROP DAM

HUNSLET RLY. BRIDGE
(L. & N. E. R.)

Waterloo Coal Staith
(T. & R. W. Bower Ltd.)

Leeds Corporation Staith

THWAITE LOCK (DISUSED)

THWAITE DAM
THWAITE MILLS
(Thos. Horn)

THWAITE BRIDGE (SWING)

Yorkshire Copper Works Ltd.
Yorkshire Tar Distillers Ltd.
Rothwell Haigh Staiths
(Messrs. J. & J. Charlesworth Ltd.)

BULLOUGH BRIDGE (SWING)

In addition to the petrol and oil depot in the Tatie Basin, there were seven other water-served depots at Hunslet and seven depots elsewhere on the A&CN in the 1930s. 400 million gallons of petroleum liquids were carried annually.

When Knostrop Cut was made in 1775, the Aire flowed south of this but by the early twentieth century it had been re-routed to the north, as shown, and a new weir had been constructed. The navigation then left the Aire at Knostrop to rejoin it, after ten miles of canal, below Kippax Locks.

A new depot was opened at Knostrop in 1958, just below the flood lock, to replace Leeds Terminus. The small Knostrop Fall lock became disused at about the same time. The never-to-be-swung Hunslet railway bridge, built in 1899 for the Great Northern Railway Company, was demolished in 1967 as the 1,800 square yard Thwaite island and its adjacent disused lock were removed thus giving an easier approach to Knostrop Fall lock for the new tankers being built for the Esso contract.

A new wharf and new access road bridge were built below Thwaite Mills as Skelton Grange power station was constructed north of both the river and canal in the 1950s.

Sulphur is being discharged to lorry by a rail-mounted grab at Hunslet in the 1930s as a tanker barge delivers petrol nearby. This wharf and one at Goodman Street, just upriver, served the industries of east Leeds for many years by handling imports of sulphur, pig iron, silver sand and other bulk cargoes. *A&CNC*

Petroleum liquids were delivered to Hunslet for much of the twentieth century and here, Whitakers' dumb tanker barge *T.P. Bullard* is amongst craft discharging at Major & Company's wharf in 1928. *Whitakers*

Whitakers' 250-ton capacity motor tank barge *Jondor* pumps off petrol at Hunslet in 1952. Between 1950 and 1954, this vessel averaged two deliveries here per week from Saltend, near Hull.

John H. Whitaker's company began dry cargo and tanker lighterage around Hull in the late nineteenth century. Before the Second World War, their A&CN work involved delivering vegetable oils to Watsons' soap works above Leeds and petrol to Majors depot at Hunslet (see page 33) using towed dumb vessels. The company's craft became more frequent visitors to the A&CN in the 1950s after it had started to change to self-propelled motor vessels. Whitakers' dry cargo activities only impinged slightly on the waterway at this time, but the company chose to abandon these and concentrate on liquid cargoes in the early 1970s. They were involved with the Esso contract of the late 1960s and became the major carrier of petroleum liquids on the A&CN in the mid-1970s after Harkers ceased to operate their tankers, many of which were subsequently purchased by Whitakers. In addition to petroleum depots at Leeds, Hunslet, Fleet, Castleford and Wakefield, they also brought oil to power stations at Skelton Grange and Ferrybridge as well as to a company sited below Ferrybridge flood lock. Whitakers also pioneered construction of 700-ton tanker barges in the 1970s at the yard of their Yorkshire Dry Dock subsidiary. Sadly, the company's fortunes have recently declined and only two of their craft are currently at work on the Humber waterways. *George Chester*

Harkers' motor tank barge *Ennerdale H* and other craft discharge petrol at Hunslet in 1965. *Jarvis Whitton*

Whitakers' *Humber Renown* is photographed tying up at Hunslet in 1986 as one of the company's sophisticated 700-ton vessels *Humber Pride* discharges a cargo beyond. Petroleum traffic to here ceased in 1988.

The 480ft x 120ft single-storey 22ft high transit shed at BTW's new depot at Knostrop is shown under construction in January 1958. When complete, eight boat berths were sited on a 600 ft long steel-piled wharf and 'up-to-date' handling equipment had been installed. A fleet of modern road vehicles succeeded the previous Dock Street-based units and provided a collection and delivery service over the whole of the West Riding, *BTW*

Illustrations featuring the puddings carrying cargoes other than coal or smokeless fuel are rare. Here, however, in the early 1960s, they are shown moored, loaded with coils of steel wire, outside Knostrop depot with a steam tug in attendance. *Waterways Museum, Goole*

In 1959, BW introduced a 'Continental Container Service' whereby plastic containers, one of which is shown here on a BW lorry, were delivered from Yorkshire factories to European and Scandinavian destinations by road to Leeds, barge to Hull or Goole and ship across the North Sea. Imports came similarly by the reverse route. The service was obstructed by dockers and wharfingers especially at Hull and had ceased by the mid-1960s. BW

Leeds Inland Port Services (LIP) were established to try to find other uses for the puddings as the smokeless fuel traffic ended. A lengthened compartment boat was made by welding together two pans that had been cut down and used to handle a 20ft container loaded with waste paper. The demonstration took place outside Knostrop depot in 1986 and is illustrated here. Little further was heard of the venture.

Hargreaves' steam tug *Aire*, purchased by the company in 1922 to replace horses, brings coal-laden dumb craft up Knostrop Cut in the 1930s, probably bound for the company's domestic coal wharf at East Street, Leeds. The vessel was scrapped in 1953. *Doug Walker*

The removal of Thwaite 'island' and Thwaite lock took place in 1967 and this view was photographed looking towards Hunslet railway bridge which was also due for demolition at the time. The 1961-mechanised Knostrop Fall lock is also visible beneath the bridge as well as the footbridge over the pre-1905 course of the River Aire. Waterloo coal staithe lies to the right. This was where craft both discharged and loaded coal in the nineteenth century and loaded it in the early twentieth century. For twenty years, ending in 1997, sewage sludge was loaded close to this point to be taken to Goole for disposal at sea. Even in 1893, Tom Bradley witnessed:

A vile floating coagulated mass of stinking impurity...

here and commented on Leeds Corporation's honeyed words attempting to mask reality in the way company spokespersons still do today. BW

An aerial view of
the 1967 removal
of Thwaite island
and its disused
lock from above
the railway bridge.
Andy Horn Collection

A general merchandise tow of by-traders boats bound for Leeds is pictured approaching
Thwaite basin in the 1910s, hauled by the A&CNC's steam tug *No 7*. This tug handled
the final tows in the 1940s. *Stan Barrass*

The steam coaster *Pioneer* lies moored at the water-powered Thwaite mills after discharging a cargo of China clay in the 1900s. Pictures of this vessel near Warehouse Hill in Leeds were taken at about the same time.

The mills were used to grind material for the pottery industry and to make whiting by grinding chalk at this time. They eventually changed over to manufacturing putty in the 1930s and continued with this until 1975 when floods destroyed the adjacent weir on the River Aire, leaving their waterwheels high and dry. *Andy Horn Collection*

BTW's diver is preparing to go down from their maintenance vessel *Salvage* outside Thwaite mills in the early 1950s as the old swing bridge was being replaced by a fixed road bridge a few feet further up the canal. The new bridge itself was replaced in the 1980s. *William Leslie Horn*

G D Holmes's motor barge *James Jones* passes beneath the new access road bridge to Thwaite mills in the early 1970s, bound for Leeds. The vessel, built in 1960 by Dunstons of Thorne, was subsequently converted to a tug after colliding with a ship on the River Trent in 1979.

The Goole-based G D Holmes company was founded in the 1890s and built up a fleet of keels and sloops involved with general cargo work but mainly with aggregate traffic, including construction of the Ouse training walls. They began to change over to motor barges in the 1930s and at the time of this photograph owned three large vessels which were sold in 1975 as the company ceased to carry, *William Horn*

With the main services bridge to Skelton Grange power station in the background, Esso Petroleum's *Esso Saltend* heads for Leeds in the 1950s. The 123ft long vessel was built in 1956 by Dunstons of Thorne. *William Horn*

Cawoods, a long-established barging company involved with sand and industrial fuels, began their final solo inland waterway work in the early 1960s delivering coal to Skelton Grange power station. They had a fleet of fourteen 200-ton capacity motor barges built by Dunstons at Thorne, one of which is shown here leaving the power station wharf to collect another cargo in 1965. *Jarvis Whitton*

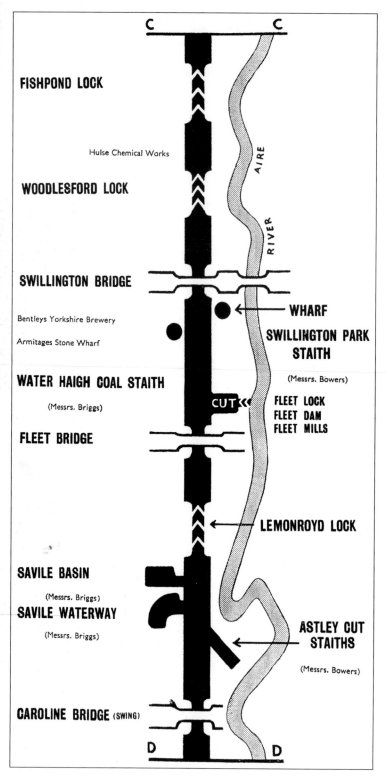

FISHPOND LOCK

Hulse Chemical Works

WOODLESFORD LOCK

C — C

A I R E

R I V E R

SWILLINGTON BRIDGE

Bentleys Yorkshire Brewery

Armitages Stone Wharf

WHARF

SWILLINGTON PARK STAITH

(Messrs. Bowers)

WATER HAIGH COAL STAITH

(Messrs. Briggs)

CUT

FLEET LOCK
FLEET DAM
FLEET MILLS

FLEET BRIDGE

LEMONROYD LOCK

SAVILE BASIN

(Messrs. Briggs)

SAVILE WATERWAY

(Messrs. Briggs)

ASTLEY CUT STAITHS

(Messrs. Bowers)

CAROLINE BRIDGE (SWING)

D — D

The 1½-mile long Cryer Cut, west of Woodlesford, was completed in 1709 and avoided a tortuous part of the River Aire's route. It is still traceable between the railway and current course of the canal. There were also pre-1800 cuts around Fleet dam and at Astley. A petrol depot was established above the disused Fleet lock before the Second World War.

This whole section was notable for the number of coal staithes on it; Briggs had three and Bowers two, in addition to Waterloo staithe on the previous section. All these staithes loaded to both puddings and by-traders' craft. The area below Lemonroyd lock was a desolate region containing several coal mines with their associated spoil heaps and 'lakes' caused by mining subsidence. To quote Tom Bradley's words from the *Yorkshire Weekly Post*:

> *We drop across an occasional bit of pastoral landscape which would be very charming were it not that we invariably find a coal pit stuck in the middle of it.*

In 1988, the Aire burst its bank and flooded the adjacent St Aidan's opencast coal mine. By 1995, a new Lemonroyd lock had been built and the river re-routed, with elimination of Kippax lock.

Fusedale H, a former Harker tanker built at Knottingley in 1967 for the Leeds Esso contract and here converted to a dry cargo barge, pens up Fishpond lock in 2001, bound for Hunslet with a cargo of aggregate. Initially in the late 1980s, deliveries were made via Leeds locks to the Tatie Basin. The operation was subsequently transferred to Hunslet and, from there to Whitwood, in 2001. *Mike Brown*

Horse-drawn L&L shortboats loaded with coal are shown penning up Woodlesford lock in the 1900s, probably bound for wharves in the Skipton area.

A Cawoods' coal barge loads at Water Haigh staithe for Skelton Grange power station in the 1960s. The colliery was some distance away, south of the main railway line. This staithe was also one of the main loading points for the puddings. *Jarvis Whitton*

A Cawoods Hargreaves push tow is seen coming down the A&CN past the site of Water Haigh staithe. Unusually, this updated Tom Pudding system, designed to deliver coal to Ferrybridge 'C' power station, here consisted of four loaded pans rather than the usual three (see later). The even number of pans was because trials for the carriage of pipes from Yorkshire Copper Works, above Fishpond lock, to Goole were taking place with the idea of resting them on coal and their lengths were such that they stretched over two units. *Norman Burnitt*

This view of the petroleum terminal's discharge berth was taken from a tanker that had just entered Fleet Cut in 1981. Regent Petroleum's original depot had fallen into disuse and been reopened in 1976.

The terminal's discharge berth had been moved out of Fleet Cut to a wharf on the main line of the navigation by 1987 when this picture was taken. It shows Whitfleet's *Fleet Enterprise*, another of the sophisticated 700-ton tankers, on the berth as the 480-ton capacity effluent tanker *Trentaire* (formerly the French vessel *Angers*) heads up to Knostrop to load.

Whitfleet, a Whitaker subsidiary, was created in 1976 and their tanker fleet subsequently delivered fuel from the Humber to Fleet depot. Another Whitaker subsidiary, the Yorkshire Dry Dock Company, based in Hull, built *Fleet Enterprise* for Whitfleet in 1983, having built a sister ship *Fleet Endeavour* in 1980.

LICS's 1961-built motor barge *No 6 Hazelwood*, purchased from Hargreaves in 1971, heads out of Lemonroyd lock in the early 1970s with coal for its owner's Leeds wharf as lock lengthening work takes place. *P L Smith*

The aftermath of the 1988 River Aire breach looking east is featured on this view, showing, from left, part of the flooded opencast mine, the river and Lemonroyd lock on the A&CN.

After the breach, the Aire was taken through a cutting alongside its former course and beside the original canal to produce a new stretch of navigation. A new Lemonroyd lock was built and this westwards-looking 1995 aerial view of its official opening shows it containing a petrol tanker bound for Fleet depot with one of the effluent tankers heading for Knostrop to load, waiting to pen up.

Hargreaves' motor barge *Katharine* is pictured loading in Savile basin with their *No 6* loaded and ready to leave in 1985, shortly before closure of the colliery after nearly a century of operation.

The Hargreaves company began as domestic coal carriers to Leeds in the early twentieth century using horse-hauled craft and, under its various subsequent titles, expanded into industrial coal, working on the A&CN, C&HN and L&LC, to LCED, the latter involving deliveries to power stations at Whitehall Road and Kirkstall. Undoubtedly, the company's greatest involvement however, was with the Ferrybridge power stations which they served from the opening of 'A' station in 1927 until 'C' finished with water transport in 2002. From the early 1920s until the early 1960s, most of Hargreaves work was undertaken by tug-hauled dumb barges from a mixed fleet of wooden and steel craft. *Katharine,* one of a group of fifteen dumb steel craft built between 1957 and 1962, was subsequently motorised at the company's Lock Lane depot at Castleford, along with most of the others. Latterly, in the interests of economy, the company worked these 240-ton capacity Dunstons-built craft in pairs with a motor barge push-towing either a dumb vessel or one with its engine out of use and this was the case at the time of this photograph.

Hargreaves' coal barge pairs are pictured entering and leaving Savile basin in 1985 with a desolate coal mining landscape visible in the background.

Astley staithe was once a rail-fed colliery loading point situated on a cut which took the original waterway back into the Aire via a lock, before Kippax lock was built in the mid-nineteenth century. The staithe fell into disuse but reopened in 1974 to handle opencast coal delivered by road from St Aidan's opencast site. Hargreaves' steel dumb barge *Santa Maria* is shown loading coal here for Ferrybridge 'B' station in the 1970s. The staithe was replaced in 1987 but had to be resited after the 1988 breach. *Hargreaves*

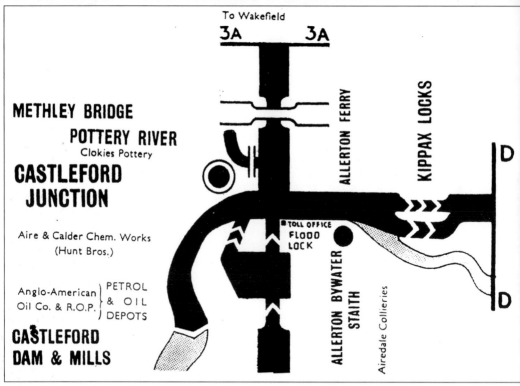

To Wakefield

3A   3A

METHLEY BRIDGE

POTTERY RIVER
Clokies Pottery

CASTLEFORD
JUNCTION

Aire & Calder Chem. Works
(Hunt Bros.)

Anglo-American } PETROL
Oil Co. & R.O.P. } & OIL
} DEPOTS

CASTLEFORD
DAM & MILLS

ALLERTON FERRY

KIPPAX LOCKS

D

■ TOLL OFFICE
FLOOD
LOCK

ALLERTON BYWATER
STAITH

Airedale Collieries

D

From the mid-nineteenth century until the flooding of 1988, the canal and river rejoined below Kippax lock. Then, with re-routing of the navigation and river, this lock was eliminated and the canal and river joined below Lemonroyd lock. To the north of Castleford, at a four-way junction, the Leeds branch meets the Wakefield branch of the A&CN and they continue together east along Castleford Cut whilst the River Aire which assimilates the Calder at the junction, heads past Castleford wharves before passing over the town weir.

This photograph was taken from the cab of a Cawoods Hargreaves push tug handling a loaded three-pan set as it approached Kippax Lock in the 1970s. A tug pulling a light pan set is approaching, bound for Astley staithe to load. Cawoods Hargreaves' modern version of the Tom Pudding operation started in 1967 with nine tugs and thirty-five compartments and was exclusively concerned with delivering coal to Ferrybridge 'C' power station, The final delivery was made from Astley in December 2002, by which time 43 million tons had been carried, most of this from collieries within a ten-mile radius of the power station.

Empty dumb barges under tow by Hargreaves' steam tug *Aire* are shown passing through Kippax lock on their way to load at one of the A&CN's staithes in 1936. The lock became disused after rerouting of the waterway following the 1988 breach. *A&CNC*

This 1930s shot shows puddings being loaded at Allerton Bywater staithe, with a horse in use for shunting pit tubs. *A&CNC*

This 1940s photograph at Allerton Bywater was taken as a loaded L&L shortboat was being towed upriver, bound for a wharf above Leeds, past a larger vessel which had just finished loading a cargo of coal. Puddings can also be seen waiting to load. The closure of this staithe, near to Leeds, in 1971 was a major blow to LICS whose craft then had to travel much further to load. *D. Wells*

This mis-captioned postcard view shows a vessel at 'four-lane ends' being manoeuvred into Castleford Cut to the left via one of the two entrances.

CENTRAL DOCKS CASTLEFORD

The effluent tanker *Trentcal* (formerly the French vessel *Auvergne*) is pictured early in 1991 at 'four-lane ends' when bound to load at Knostrop.

Craft are pictured in the 1930s moored outside Hunt Brothers' chemical works, a few hundred yards above Castleford weir. There was a petrol depot close by and grain was delivered by water to a mill adjacent to the weir which is still in use.

CHAPTER TWO

Calder Mouth to Wakefield and Beyond

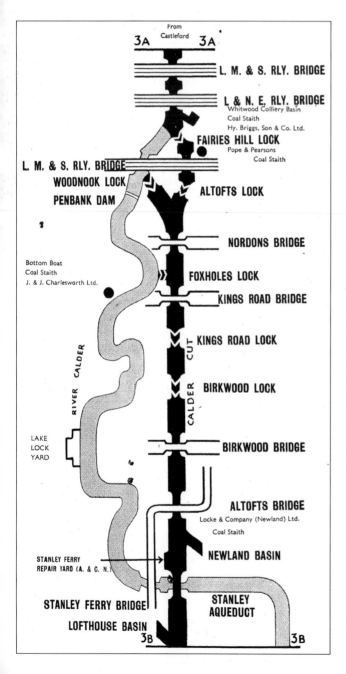

From Castleford

3A   3A

L. M. & S. RLY. BRIDGE

L & N. E. RLY. BRIDGE
Whitwood Colliery Basin
Coal Staith
Hy. Briggs, Son & Co. Ltd.

FAIRIES HILL LOCK
Pope & Pearsons
Coal Staith

L. M. & S. RLY. BRIDGE
WOODNOOK LOCK   ALTOFTS LOCK
PENBANK DAM

NORDONS BRIDGE

Bottom Boat
Coal Staith
J. & J. Charlesworth Ltd.   FOXHOLES LOCK

KINGS ROAD BRIDGE

KINGS ROAD LOCK

RIVER CALDER   CALDER CUT

BIRKWOOD LOCK

LAKE
LOCK
YARD   BIRKWOOD BRIDGE

ALTOFTS BRIDGE
Locke & Company (Newland) Ltd.
Coal Staith

STANLEY FERRY   NEWLAND BASIN
REPAIR YARD (A. & C. N.)

STANLEY FERRY BRIDGE   STANLEY
                         AQUEDUCT
LOFTHOUSE BASIN
3B   3B

Four-lane ends, near Castleford (page 55), is the eastern extremity of the A&CNC's Wakefield branch.

Several coal loading staithes are shown and also the sites of two of the four locks on the original river route to Wakefield. These were adjacent to dams at Penbank and the A&CNC's 1802-built Lake Lock yard. Improvements took place in the vicinity of both these locks early in the nineteenth century but, by 1839, they had both been by-passed by the four and a half-mile long Calder Cut between Fairies Hill lock and Broad Reach flood lock, which included utilisation of Stanley Ferry aqueduct, completed in 1839. This reduced the previous waterway route between Wakefield and Castleford by five miles. In 1873, activities at Lake Lock yard, where the A&CNC's craft had been maintained and built at a rate of one per month since the mid-1860s, were transferred to a recently purchased yard at Stanley Ferry that had been established by a private company in the 1850s.

Wakefield traffic was routed via Woodnook lock in the 1950s because Fairies Hill and Altofts locks had become disused after coal ceased to be loaded on the canal between them. Altofts lock was filled in but Fairies Hill has been reopened recently to serve a marina above the lock. In 1981, a replacement aqueduct was built at Stanley Ferry and Whitwood basin was developed to become the site of a new aggregate wharf, opened in 2001.

Pottery River or Whitwood Mere was part of the old course of the Calder and once supported several glass and pottery manufacturers. This aerial view shows industrial premises sited on the Castleford bank and the junction with the Wakefield branch of the A&CN. Horse-drawn craft delivered coal and sand here until the Second World War. *T Young*

This advertisement for one of the Whitwood Mere factories uses an etching showing craft, including a sailing sloop, on the mere.

THE MEAR GLASS BOTTLE WORKS,
WHITWOOD, CASTLEFORD,

An A&C general merchandise tow heads down the Calder towards Castleford in the 1920s. The tug/barge is hauling a train of six dumb barges. This illustration was one of a pair that were used on a postcard published by the A&CNC contrasting this modern way of moving craft with the old fashioned method of horse haulage featured on a picture of the S&SYN.

Workmen standing on stout planks, supported at one end by the maintenance boat *Vulcan* and stonework on the canal bank at the other, are raising four loaded puddings that had sunk, chained together, in Whitwood colliery basin in 1958. They were lying 5ft beneath the water and screw jacks were in use to lift each pan and its contents, weighing about 50 tons, to the surface so that the craft could then be pumped out. The whole operation took four days. *Ken Ramsden*

Hornshaws' former BTW motor barge *Gladys Lillian*, launched at Dunstons' Thorne yard in 1957, is shown in January 2003 discharging a cargo of Trent aggregate at Lafarge's wharf, built by widening the former Whitwood colliery basin.

Harkers' tanker barge *Berriedale H* enters Woodnook lock in the early 1960s, bound for Wakefield with a cargo of fuel oil. *P L Smith*

LICS's steam tug *Unity*, is shown stranded in Woodnook lock after the lock's lower gates gave way, draining the pound. The tug was hauling empty barges to Parkhill colliery to load in 1953. *Unity* continued in service until 1958. *D&IWE*

Foxholes (Papworth's) lock was built to give access from Calder Cut to both Bottom Boat coal staithe and the A&CNC's Lake Lock yard. This postcard view of the lock shows craft waiting to pass through into the Calder and load coal in the 1900s. The lock was built with four pairs of gates enabling it to be used whether the river level was above or below that in the canal. It was closed in 1962 having served as the only access to the former route of the navigation for several years.

Bottom Boat staithe was fed since 1804 by the four-mile long Lake Lock railroad which originally met the river at Lake Lock. Puddings began loading here in 1897 and activity ended just after the Second World War. A&CNC men are shown on a tour of inspection during the mid-1940s coming down the old course of the A&CN with the derelict staithe in the background. *Alan Hall Collection*

Hargreaves motor barges *Ann* and *Joyce* leave the nearby lock and approach King's Road bridge loaded with coal from Parkhill, bound for Ferrybridge 'B' power station in 1979. Whitakers' *Marchdale*, loaded with oil for Wakefield, waits to pen up. The typical A&C replacement bridge was built and the waterway widened in the 1860s (see 1867 in Chronology, page 8).

A train of puddings hauled by steam tug has just crossed Stanley Ferry aqueduct as a light vessel waits to head towards Wakefield in the opposite direction in this 1950s photograph. A steam dredger lies outside Stanley Ferry yard to the right and the entrance to Newland basin is just visible on the opposite bank. Stanley Ferry yard remains an important BW depot, specialising in the construction of lock gates. *BW*

An unusual method of loading puddings was practised in Newland basin between 1891 and 1939. Some were loaded conventionally at a staithe, but others were floated onto rail transporters and hauled out of the water to be taken along standard gauge track, by one of the two saddle-tank locomotives based here, to St John's colliery screens, about a mile away. A compartment is shown after loading in the 1930s, ready to be returned to the water on this much-used posed photograph. The buffers and fittings enabling pans to be chained together when under tow on the A&CN may be seen, together with the stempost which fitted into a recess on the pan in front. *John Goodchild Collection*

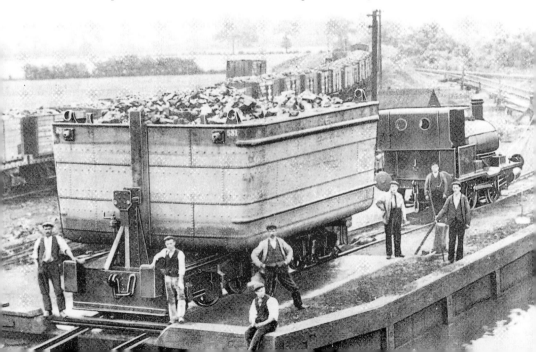

A de-watered Stanley Ferry aqueduct receives a general overhaul in 1936. The water box of the cast iron suspension aqueduct, designed by George Leather, was held by rods from two bowstring girders supported on stone abutments. *A West*

Stanley Ferry aqueduct suffered occasional impact damage from passing craft during both the nineteenth and twentieth centuries. Also, some suspension rods were found to carry no weight whilst others were overloaded. As a consequence, It was decided to build a replacement a short distance upriver and this was slid into position from one bank as shown on this advertisement published shortly after the 1981 event. The project was described by the company:

A new pre-cast concrete trough was built on site and launched into its final position by a magnificently orchestrated six day hydraulic push.

This 1983 view from an oil tanker bound for Wakefield shows the vessel lining up to cross the new aqueduct with the old structure, to the right, out of use.

Two A&CNC flyboats were swept over Kirkthorpe dam when a rope broke as they were being towed out of Broad Reach flood lock into the Calder whilst en route for Wakefield in 1931. The vessels were recovered by floating them downriver to Stanley Ferry where they were hauled up ramps onto the top of the river bank and relaunched into the canal. *No 112* is shown prior to relaunching, along with the large gang necessary to accomplish such a procedure. *A&CNC*

Lofthouse basin saw many puddings being loaded from rail-fed staithes until 1924. Coal then continued to be loaded here using lorry-fed staithes, one of which is visible on this 1974 photograph taken as a cargo of cotton was being discharged from Flixborough Shipping's 350-ton capacity motor barge *Thealby* during the basin's reactivation between 1960 and 1977.

(Old petrol tankers moored in the basin had served as a storage depot for waterborne supplies of oil in the early 1960s.) Flixborough Shipping Company were founded in 1940 to bring coal for coking from south and west Yorkshire collieries to Scunthorpe steel works using the S&SYN as well as the A&CN. Initially, Sheffield size ($61^{1}/_{2}$ft x $15^{1}/_{2}$ft) craft were bought and built, but in the late 1960s they had larger vessels constructed by Harkers, such as *Thealby*, launched in 1973. The company finished trading in the 1980s. *Thealby*, renamed *Tirley*, subsequently worked on the River Severn waterways for over a decade, delivering grain to a mill at Tewkesbury. *P L Smith*

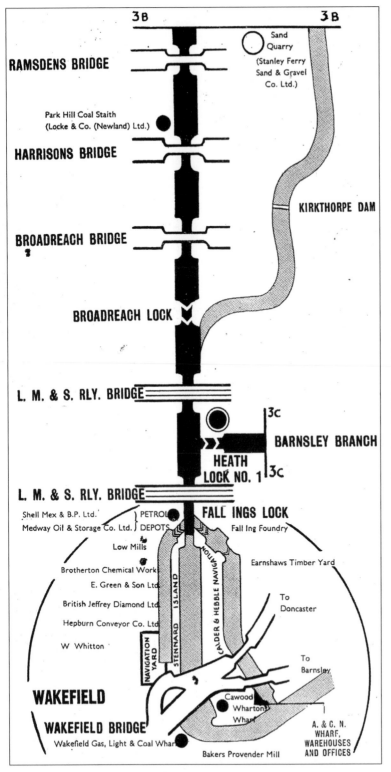

The other locks on the original river route between Calder Mouth and Wakefield were at Kirkthorpe dam and Wakefield. The former was eliminated by construction of Calder Cut, whilst the latter, at the junction of the Calder with the old mill weir (Old Cut) on which the former A&CNC head offices were sited between 1821 and 1851, remained in use until finally being abandoned after the Second World War.

Heath entrance lock, linking the River Calder to the Barnsley Canal which the A&CNC had purchased in 1875, is shown on the strip map. The A&CNC lengthened locks on the Canal but transhipment to smaller craft still took place in the river at Heath during the late-eighteenth and early twentieth centuries as vessels too large to use the waterway brought cargoes of woodpulp loaded at Hull for delivery to Barnsley.

Fall Ings lock, across the river from the entrance to the Old Cut, gave access to other A&CNC properties in Wakefield as well as those at Brighouse, Huddersfield and Dewsbury. In the late 1870s, the A&CNC had bought the derelict Savile Cut, near Dewsbury, and built a timber warehouse and canal basin on it to add to the extension they had added in 1865 to the 1778-built warehouse at Huddersfield.

In the 1880s, the A&CNC built Calder Row, brick-built terraced housing on the canal bank near Stanley Ferry, to house their employees. It lies in the background of this 1987 photograph of a Hargreaves pair bound for Ferrybridge 'B' power station with, amazingly, Australian coal imported via Keadby on the Trent, lorried to Wakefield and loaded to barge there.

Hargreaves' motor barge *Katharine* loads coal at Parkhill staithe in 1979. The staithe and adjacent colliery opened in 1877 and closed in 1982.

One regular cargo delivered to Barnsley in the first half of the twentieth century, was woodpulp for the paper mills. This is being discharged in 1912, using a Telfer, the driver of which is holding an infant! Apart from an A&CNC steam flyboat service which ended in the early 1920s, the Barnsley Canal was exclusive to horse-hauled craft until the 1940s. Horses and accompanying horse marines were usually hired at Wakefield.

Humber Keel & Sloop Preservation Society

A light vessel waits in the River Calder against the closed bottom gates of Heath lock to enter the Barnsley Canal in the 1900s. Cog boats which were towed by dumb craft to be used for various off-vessel operations, have been left here for safe-keeping whilst cargoes are delivered to Barnsley. Roger Glister's book, *The Forgotten Canals of Yorkshire (Swinton to Wakefield via Barnsley)* to be published by Wharncliffe Books, describes both the Barnsley and Dearne & Dove Canals.

The end came for the Barnsley Canal in November 1946 with a major breach at Littleworth, shown here. For years, subsidence of the canal had been treated by adding pit spoil to the towpath, thereby raising the banks which eventually became unstable. *D&IWE*

Puddings are being loaded at a lorry-fed staithe just above the railway bridge during the 1950s in the shadow of Wakefield power station cooling towers, built near the former entrance to the Barnsley Canal. *D&IWE*

This 1952 picture shows a former A&CNC steam flyboat visiting Heath lock to remove the lockkeeper's furniture after the canal had been abandoned. *Stan Barrass*

On the River Calder, facing upstream, Whitakers' *Keewhit* delivers fuel oil at Wakefield in 1980. This vessel was built by the Yorkshire Dry Dock Company at Hull in 1955, lengthened from 104½ft to 127ft in the late 1950s and then followed the opposite path from several craft pictured in this book in being converted from a dry cargo barge to a tanker.

This etching by Henry Clarke, dating from the late 1880s depicts a vessel on the Old Mill Goit at Wakefield; the original route of the A&CN at Wakefield. *John Goodchild Collection*

E. Green & Sons' 'Economiser' works were one of the last users of the Old Cut at Wakefield and a vessel is shown waiting in the 1920s to load one of their products for delivery to Hull, or perhaps Salford, for export. This stretch of the A&CN, accessed via a small (64ft x 14½ft) lock, was last used commercially in the early 1940s. *Waterways Museum, Goole*

The A&CNC had warehouses on the C&HN at Wakefield and the motor barge *Valour BW* is shown tied up there after discharging a cargo in the late 1950s. *Waterways Museum, Goole*

Until the mid-twentieth century, the A&CNC kept horses at both Dewsbury and Wakefield to haul their craft on the C&HN. Two of the animals and their handlers dealing with Brighouse, Cooper Bridge and Huddersfield traffics are shown here at Double Locks, near Dewsbury.

From the mid-nineteenth century to the mid-twentieth century, the A&CNC owned warehouses at Dewsbury, Cooper Bridge, Brighouse and Huddersfield. All were reached by 58ft x 14ft (West Country size) A&CNC flyboats using the C&HN. Additionally, craft trading to the premises shown above Wakefield Road Bridge at Huddersfield, would have had to use the Huddersfield Broad Canal, visible beyond the bridge.

CHAPTER THREE

Castleford to Ferrybridge

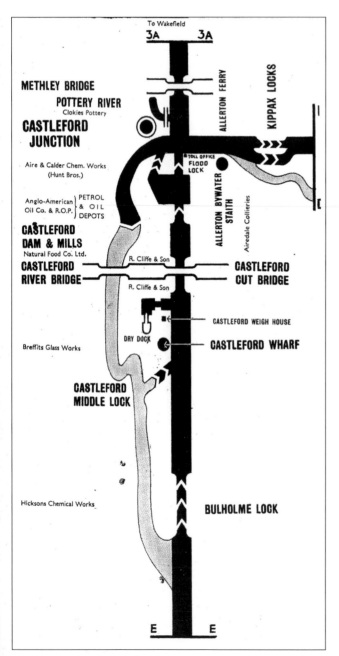

Castleford Cut has been one of the busiest stretches of the A&CN ever since it was opened in 1775 to replace the original 1700 cut built merely to by-pass the weir. It was entered in the 1930s at its western end from 'four-lane ends' by either a small flood lock or by a much larger flood basin with gates at each end.

The canal bank on the south side, immediately above and below the road bridge, was the base of a shipbuilder and repairer until acquired by Hargreaves in the 1950s. In the 1980s, an oil depot was established above the bridge and this was reopened in 2002 by a company which promised to deliver to it by water.

Until Bulholme lock was opened in 1828, traffic entered the lower end of Castleford Cut from the Aire via Castleford Middle lock. After this lock had become disused during the Second World War, a lorry-fed staithe was built on the site and puddings began loading smokeless fuel here in the 1960s until this ceased in 1980 leaving collection of this cargo from Doncaster on the S&SYN to continue for a few more years.

Canal and river rejoin below Bulholme lock and the 'five-mile pond' to Ferrybridge begins. Lockkeepers' cottages here have been built on stilts to lift them above the river's flood level.

A pudding tug enters Castleford flood lock at the head of Castleford Cut in the 1900s, as other vessels wait to follow. In the nineteenth century the Toll Officer here could drop a chain in front of any vessel whose captain failed to give satisfactory answers to his questions and, until well into the twentieth century, there were delays here as tolls were collected. A horse ferry operated across the Aire from the flood lock for Calder traffic until the 1940s.

Whitakers' 700-ton tanker barge *Humber Pride*, returning light from Hunslet in 1987, makes extensive use of its power whilst passing through Castleford flood lock.

Castleford flood lock is shown drained for maintenance in 1966, with stop planks in the foreground. By this time, the small flood lock, out of shot to the right of this view, had become disused. BW

On this busy 1951 scene at Castleford, Fred Acaster's Manvers size (58½ft x 15ft) *Bessie* and a larger light craft head out of the flood lock into Castleford Cut. On occasions in the early 1930s, *Bessie* delivered a cargo of imported sand from Goole via the S&SYN and Dearne & Dove Canal to glassworks at Barnsley. Subsequently, the barge loaded coal on the Barnsley Canal before returning to Goole using the A&CN.
Passage around this 'Yorkshire Ring' became impossible after the Dearne & Dove Canal was closed in the early 1930s. Another A&CNC 1867-built replacement bridge over a widened waterway may be seen in the background. *D&IWE*

Looking up Castleford Cut towards the flood lock from the road bridge over it in the 1950s, loaded and light pudding trains are seen passing each other. Note the differing positions of the jebus on each tow.
D&IWE

The keel *Waverley* and guests are posed outside Richard Cliffe's yard adjacent to the bridge over Castleford Cut, shortly after its launching in 1900. The vessel was built for Mark Holgate of Beverley. It was commandeered and towed to France during the First World War, never to be seen again.
Raymond Tattersall Collection

This 1940s view from the bridge over Castleford Cut looks past Richard Cliffe's yard towards Bulholme lock. A variety of craft are visible including Hargreaves' steam tug *Audrey* with dumb barge in tow, and a steam pudding tug plus pans. Castleford weigh house into which new vessels were taken to be calibrated is visible to the right. Both these premises and the adjacent yard of Richard Cliffe were taken over by Hargreaves in the 1950s to become the base of their coal carrying business with the dry dock being used for repair, maintenance and the 1960s motorising of their dumb craft. Later, the Cawoods Hargreaves Ferrybridge 'C' tows were also managed from here. *A&CNC*

Just visible on the previous photograph is Castleford Middle Lock, shown here in the 1900s on a view looking down the cut towards Bulholme lock with merchandise tug *No 3* moored close to the upper lock gates. The lock remained in use until the 1940s.

A lorry-fed loading staithe was built in the mid-1940s on the site of Castleford Middle lock after this had become disused. Pans are being loaded with smokeless fuel here in the 1970s.

Old and new compartment boats are shown at Castleford in 1967 as Cawoods Hargreaves' *CH 105* pulls a three-pan train past the Tom Pudding loading staithe towards Bulholme lock. Coamings are visible on some of the puddings moored there, enabling them to carry cargoes other than coal which needed to be covered. *Norman Burnitt*

Hargreaves diesel tug *Elsa Margareta*, built by the Yorkshire Dry Dock Company at Hull in 1958, is shown at work on Castleford Cut. In 1961, the company decided to motorise their dumb craft and the tug was sold to an Immingham company, Hargreaves.

Bulholme lock is shown in the 1930s, illustrating the intermediate gates and 460ft length, able to accommodate a nineteen-pan pudding train. Other single craft could pen through at the same time using the embayment, here containing the A&CNC wooden steam flyboat *No 18,* built at Stanley Ferry yard. The other steam flyboat surviving after nationalisation was *No 38.* Both vessels were 80ft x 14½ft and carried up to 80 tons of cargo with a crew of three. During the 1940s, they carried flour and cement between Hull and Leeds or Wakefield, with an occasional delivery of ground maize to Tetleys' wharf at Leeds. *A&CNC*

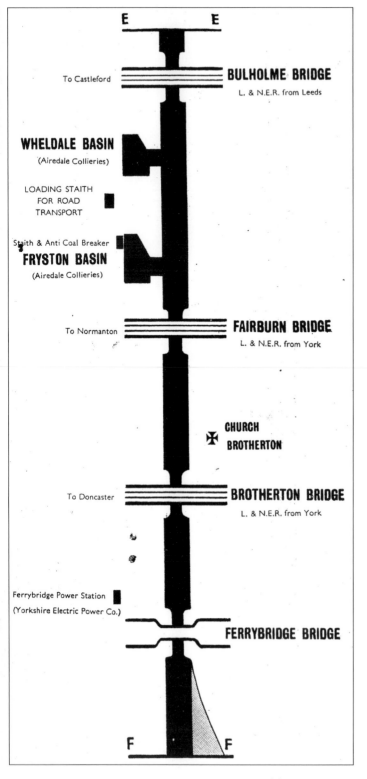

E   E

To Castleford

BULHOLME BRIDGE

L. & N.E.R. from Leeds

WHELDALE BASIN

(Airedale Collieries)

LOADING STAITH
FOR ROAD
TRANSPORT

Staith & Anti Coal Breaker

FRYSTON BASIN

(Airedale Collieries)

To Normanton

FAIRBURN BRIDGE

L. & N.E.R. from York

✠ **CHURCH
BROTHERTON**

To Doncaster

BROTHERTON BRIDGE

L. & N.E.R. from York

Ferrybridge Power Station

(Yorkshire Electric Power Co.)

FERRYBRIDGE BRIDGE

F   F

Below Castleford Cut lies the 'five-mile pond', a stretch of the River Aire, much improved in appearance from the industrial desolation of the mid-to late-twentieth century caused by spoil heaps of colliery waste, subsequently flattened and then waterlogged after mining subsidence. The varying scales of these strip maps may be appreciated by comparing the five miles represented here with the two miles on page 74.

The two colliery basins, opened in 1870 (Wheldale) and 1894 (Fryston), were closed in the 1980s.

There were short canals, all opened and closed in the first half of the nineteenth century, at Fairburn and Brotherton for export of material from nearby quarries.

Three power stations were constructed on the south bank between Brotherton and the Great North Road bridge at Ferrybridge, now an ancient monument replaced by a 1967-built overpass. Coal was delivered by water to all of them. Listed moving downstream, they were Ferrybridge 'C', opened in 1967, Ferrybridge 'B', 1957-91, and Ferrybridge 'A', 1927-75. This stretch of water was always prone to fog formation. Craft were eventually able to contact locks and other vessels in the vicinity by VHF radio, thereby reducing the risk of accidents. Surprisingly, Hargreaves and Cawoods Hargreaves were the last operators to fit this facility in 1987.

A Cawoods Hargreaves tug shunts loaded pans in Wheldale basin, days before its closure in 1987.

A pudding loaded via an anti-breakage device in Fryston basin is pictured in the 1930s.

Waterways Museum, Goole

Horse haulage of short-haul coal traffic lasted on the A&CN until the Second World War and facilities were provided to ferry the animals across the waterway wherever the towpath changed sides. A horse and handler are shown being sculled away from Fryston basin in the 1940s on the ferry based at Bulholme lock. Similar ferries also existed at Calder Mouth, Kippax and Thwaite at this time.
Jack Hulme

Hargreaves motor barge *No 5* leaves Fryston basin for the River Aire in 1983 after collecting a cargo of coal for Ferrybridge 'B' power station.

A loaded Cawoods Hargreaves three-pan set carrying over 500 tons of coal heads into the channel leading to the hoist serving Ferrybridge 'C' power station in the 1980s.

A loaded pan is lifted for tipping at the Ferrybridge 'C' hoist in the 1980s.

Loaded Hargreaves' dumb barges are pictured in the 1950s waiting in the river outside Ferrybridge 'B' power station to be discharged. *Hargreaves*

This photograph, taken in 1946 from the top of Brotherton church tower before 'B' and 'C' power stations were built, shows a train of Hargreaves' coal barges passing downriver, bound for Ferrybridge 'A' power station, under tow by the company's steam tug *Audrey*. *Hargreaves*

A loaded pudding train passes an upriver general merchandise tow beneath Brotherton railway bridge on this view dating from the 1910s.

Hargreaves' steam tug *Audrey*, acquired in 1940, tows one of the company's empty dumb barges away from Ferrybridge 'A' power station wharf in the 1940s. Unloading at 'A' and 'B' stations was by conventional grabs. *Audrey* was scrapped in the 1950s. *Hargreaves*

Hargreaves motor tug/barge *Lawson,* acquired in 1942, tows the 83½ft x 16½ft dumb barges *Susan* and *Topsy* away from Ferrybridge 'A' wharf after their naming ceremony in 1957. The barges were subsequently motorised by the company. *Hargreaves*

This famous etching by N. Whittock dating from c.1830 shows John Carr's 1804-built Great North Road bridge at Ferrybridge. *Ron Gosney Collection*

Freed from the restriction of making smoke as it passed through Knottingley, the A&CNC tug/barge *No 11* hauls its tow of general merchandise craft upriver towards Ferrybridge bridge in August 1931.
Ron Gosney Collection

With Ferrybridge 'A' power station in the background, Harkers' tanker barge *Elsie H*, unusually heading upriver light, is shown in 1953 photographed from the flood lock.
Alan Hall Collection

CHAPTER FOUR

Ferrybridge to Points on the Tideway

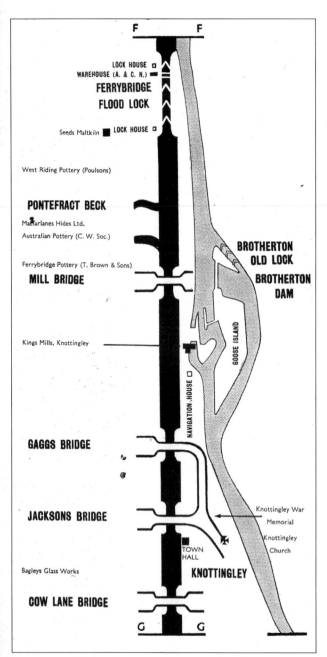

The eighteen-mile long Knottingley & Goole Canal, opened in 1826 between Ferrybridge and Goole is still part of the present route of the A&CN. Prior to 1700, Knottingley, where a weir blocked the Aire at its tidal limit, was the highest point on the River Aire to which craft could trade, thus making the town a seaport. Formation of the A&CNC in the late seventeenth century, charged with producing a navigable waterway from Weeland to Leeds and Wakefield, led to construction of Brotherton lock and cut in 1699, giving small craft access to Castleford and above. Other locks built at Beal and Haddlesey then prevented sea-going craft from reaching Knottingley and caused Rawcliffe and Airmyn, close to the Aire's confluence with the Ouse, to become important transhipment points until the Selby Canal was opened in 1778.

It has been estimated that over 1,000 wooden vessels, including more than 330 sea-going craft, were built alongside Knottingley's river and canal in the nineteenth century and this activity continued well into the twentieth century. Until the 1940s, much burnt lime and limestone were exported from the town by water. Glassworks, users of both this mineral and sand, were established alongside the canal in the nineteenth century, becoming, and in some cases remaining, involved with carriage of raw materials by barge for over a century. Potteries at both Ferrybridge and Knottingley also used the A&CN for import of raw materials and export of finished goods.

The ex-petroleum liquids tanker *Dunlin*, built at Wivenhoe by James W Cook & Company, its former owners, is shown loaded with effluent sludge from Knostrop heading into Ferrybridge flood lock in 1985. The long-established *Golden Lion* pub, once the shipping and receiving house for goods sent up and down the river by boat, lies to the right whilst the River Aire flows towards the weir and King's Mill, visible in the distance.

Looking back from the top of King's Mill towards the Ferrybridge power stations and the replacement Great North Road bridge as reconstruction work on the mill dam was taking place and the river being re-routed in 1976, the site of Brotherton old lock and cut may be seen in the foreground. The original A&CNC lock cuts were made in 1700 merely to allow boats to by-pass an existing weir. An additional lock was built between the river and a cut passing south of King's Mill in 1804. *Ron Gosney Collection*

Knottingley's old port area around Aire Street is shown on this etching, made looking west in 1846, twenty years after opening of the Knottingley & Goole Canal. By this time only cows and small ferryboats were to be seen in and on the river, apart from the towing path built along man-made mid-river islands. *Ron Gosney Collection*

This postcard view of Ferrybridge flood lock in the 1920s, looking out towards the River Aire, shows the lift bridge used by men and horses to cross the waterway. The inlet to the left, led to a small dock with adjacent warehouses, where cargoes for the locality were discharged in the days when the lift bridge and lock fitments were manually operated.

This 1980s view along the length of the now mechanised Ferrybridge flood lock with a replacement footbridge in place, shows BW's push tug *Freight Pioneer* taking their then dumb barge *Lady Kerr* through the lock, en route for Knostrop.

James Barraclough & Company's motor barge *Maranne* is shown discharging grain by suction elevator at King's Mill, Knottingley, in the 1960s. Despite the A&CNC having statutory rights to the water, there were problems in the river here for most of the eighteenth century as the millers lowered water levels by use of machinery until the A&CNC bought the mill in the 1770s. Barracloughs were the major sloop owners on the Humber waterways during the first half of the twentieth century. They began operating motor barges in the 1930s and the 200-ton capacity *Maranne* was one of their earliest. The company ceased trading in 1975. *Waterways Museum, Goole*

The front cover of this book features Norman Burnitt's photograph of a Cawoods Hargreaves three-pan push tow viewed from atop King's Mill as it heads through Knottingley cutting, to Ferrybridge 'C' with coal from Kellingley colliery. The diesel pudding tug *Brodsworth* passes through the same cutting in the 1960s bound for Goole as a loaded petrol tanker approaches King's Mill. *V Dickenson*

This early twentieth century postcard view of the canal from Jackson's Bridge at Knottingley, was taken looking towards Goole as a horse-drawn wooden vessel passed the old limestone-loading staithes. A steam tug was on the move outside Bagleys' glassworks. Branfords' yard is just visible on the opposite bank above the tug's funnel.

An aerial view which shows Bagleys' Knottingley glassworks in the 1970s, after Rockware had taken over the premises. Cow Lane Bridge is also visible.

The present John Branford's great grandfather was a mariner. John's grandfather served a seven-year apprenticeship at a Knottingley yard and eventually took over a boatyard on the land between the glassworks and Cow Lane Bridge, building barges and sea-going craft between the 1870s and 1916. He was also engaged in carrying by barge at this time. John's father, Cyril, operated a fleet of inland waterway vessels under the trading name Branford Brothers until the other two brothers retired. John himself began barging as a 15-year old in the 1960s and joined his father in 1970 on Branfords' long-lived contract delivering sand to Bagleys glassworks at Knottingley. The company then bought three ex-Harker tankers, converted to carry approximately 300 tons of dry cargo, in the 1970s. When Cyril died in 1981, John formed Branford Barge Owners and his son Jonathan eventually joined him in the aggregate trade, now based at Whitwood. The company purchased their largest vessel, the former Whitaker tanker *Humber Renown* in 1998 and converted this to a 500-ton dry cargo carrier (see page 35). Since then two more similar craft, *Farndale* and *Fossdale*, have been bought for conversion.

Rockware

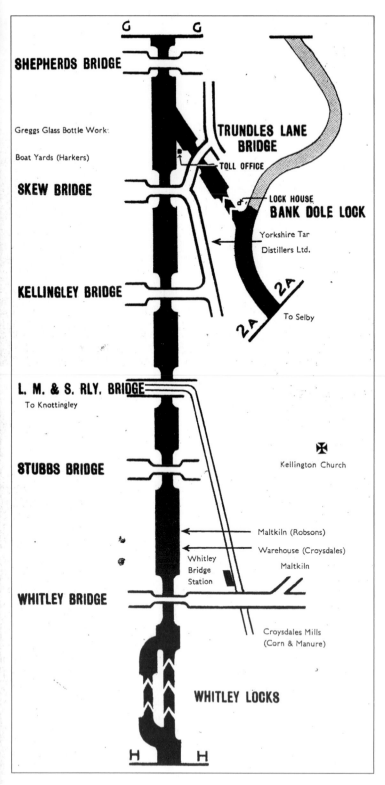

SHEPHERDS BRIDGE

Greggs Glass Bottle Work:

Boat Yards (Harkers)

SKEW BRIDGE

KELLINGLEY BRIDGE

TRUNDLES LANE BRIDGE

TOLL OFFICE

LOCK HOUSE
BANK DOLE LOCK

Yorkshire Tar
Distillers Ltd.

To Selby

L. M. & S. RLY. BRIDGE
To Knottingley

STUBBS BRIDGE

Kellington Church

Maltkiln (Robsons)

Warehouse (Croysdales)

Whitley
Bridge
Station

Maltkiln

WHITLEY BRIDGE

Croysdales Mills
(Corn & Manure)

WHITLEY LOCKS

Immediately below Shepherd's Bridge, Bank Dole Cut forks off, leading via a lock into the River Aire and thence to the Selby Canal. Tar distillation was started in 1875 alongside this stretch and the premises continued to be water-served when Yorkshire Tar Distillers took over in 1926. The company imported from waterside gasworks on York's River Foss, the A&CN, C&HN and S&SYN and also exported to Goole for onward carriage by ship. Barges still delivered to the premises until recently after Croda Hydrocarbons had subsequently acquired the plant.

When the map was drawn, Harkers' shipyard lay on the main line of the navigation. Here, the company built their own petroleum tankers and other steel craft for a variety of owners. Two earlier yards on the site were owned by Worfolks and Garlicks respectively and specialised in building wooden vessels.

In the 1960s, Kellingley colliery and staithe were opened on the north bank of the canal, about a mile below Skew Bridge. Millions of tons of coal were carried by water from here to the Ferrybridge power stations. In 2002, however, the mineral was declared to be too sulphurous, deliveries to 'C' station, which remains operational, ceased and the staithe closed.

Harkers' diesel tug *Lion*, built by them in 1931, and dumb tanker barge *Darius* are moored below Knottingley's Shepherd's Bridge in 1949. *Lion* was built longer than shown here to provide accommodation for crews of the petrol tankers it was towing who were not allowed to live aboard their own craft for safety reasons. *Jarvis Whitton*

Harkers' sea-going tanker *Constance H,* built at Knottingley in 1930, waits to pass beneath Trundles Lane bridge and reach the tar works beyond. This stone-arched bridge was typical of those replaced on the main line in the 1860s. *Harkers*

Mission accomplished as *Constance H* prepares to tie up outside the tar works to load. *Harkers*

Harkers' steam tug *As 151*, later to be renamed *Barrow*, lies tied up outside the tar works shortly after its sale by and delivery from French owners in the mid-1920s. The tug was subsequently stationed at Hunslet and used mainly for steaming heavy oil heating coils there. Part of one of Harkers' narrowboats is also visible. *Ron Gosney Collection*

Three of Whitakers' ex-Harker tankers *Marchdale H, Moredale H* and *Cotterdale H* are shown in 1979, shortly after arrival at Knottingley tar works with imported tar transhipped at Goole.

Across Bank Dole Cut from the tar works, on the site of a former ready-mixed concrete plant, Steetleys established, in 1981, a storage and distribution depot at Knottingley for aggregate delivered by water. Branfords' *Cordale* is shown being discharged to lorry at the depot in the mid-1980s. Activities were transferred to Leeds at the end of the decade and the depot closed in 1990. *Andy Horn*

This photograph shows Bank Dole lock under water during the floods of 1947. Harkers laid up their out-of-work tankers in the river beyond the lock at the time and *Ernest H* is visible to the right of the view. *Jarvis Whitton*

The L&L shortboat *Self Help* was launched in June 1900 from Garlicks' yard at Knottingley. The vessel was built for J Noble of Leeds to be used in the sand and coal traffic on both the L&LC and A&CN. Garlicks acquired the yard from Thomas Cliffe whose son Richard became established at Castleford (see page 77) in 1851. *Ron Gosney Collection*

In 1870, Worfolks' shipyard was established above and adjacent to Skew Bridge on the main line of the canal at Knottingley. A row of houses in Aimwell Place separated this yard from that of Garlicks'. Worfolks' yard, Aimwell Place and the Toll Offices across the canal, where towing horses could once be hired and stabled, may be seen on this postcard from the 1900s. *Ron Gosney Collection*

Both Garlicks' and Worfolks' yards were acquired by Harkers, the former in 1929 and the latter in 1942, after being leased since the mid-1930s. Aimwell Place was eventually demolished but not before this picture was taken. A vessel is under construction on the former Worfolk site with one of the 127ft long Dutch 'skems' lying alongside. *Ron Gosney Collection*

The coastal tanker *William Kipping* was the first motor vessel to be built at Harkers and was launched in 1929. It is shown here nearing completion on the former Garlick slipway. *Ron Gosney Collection*

The final tanker to be built by Harkers at Knottingley was *Conveyor*, seen being launched in October 1979. The vessel entered service with its new owners on the Thames in February 1980. Over 300 commercial craft were built at the yard between 1929 and 1979, including dry cargo vessels,tugs, trawlers and craft for the war effort, as well as tankers. *Harkers*

This aerial view of Harkers' yard in the 1950s from above the tar works shows the absence of Aimwell Place and the presence of a three-tanker capacity maintenance slipway that had been constructed on the opposite bank, here occupied by two craft. *Ribblesdale H* is under construction at the Worfolk end of the yard, prior to a broadside launch, as *Rosedale H* and other vessels are being fitted out whilst moored alongside the yard.

As well as the building of new craft for themselves and others, the Harker tanker fleet was repaired and maintained here, dumb boats were motorised, craft lengthened and redundant tankers converted to dry cargo craft for sale. The Harker carrying side reached a peak in the 1950s but had ceased to trade by 1976 with much of its former work and several of its craft being taken over by Whitakers. *Harkers*

Hargreaves' barges and a Cawoods Hargreaves pan set lie moored at Kellingley colliery staithe in February 1983. This was the only coal-loading staithe in regular use for Ferrybridge 'C' east of the power station.

Branfords' converted ex-Harker tanker *Mossdale* pushes their recently acquired lighter *Claire* up the A&CN past Kellingley staithe in the 1980s. Both vessels were loaded with sand for Rockware glassworks at Knottingley. *Andy Horn*

Harkers' *Glaisdale H*, recently launched from their yard at Knottingley, is shown below Kellingley in 1961 heading down to Goole to be fitted out. This procedure often had to be undertaken in the 1960s and 1970s as larger coastal tankers with fixed superstructures were being built by the company. After completion, these craft needed greater headroom than that provided by bridges over the A&CN between Knottingley and Goole, so could not be finished off at their builders' yard. *Jarvis Whitton*

A passing pleasure cruiser is shown below Kellingley in 1979 at the moment of impact with a large wave generated by the skipper of a petrol tanker in a hurry to get back to Goole. One second later, the small vessel was almost overturned before being lost to view in a spray of water.

A view from Whitley Bridge in February 1970 as Cory's tanker barge *Battle Stone* heads towards the mill wharf and lock whilst returning from Esso's Leeds depot. The mill closed in 1974 and was then used for storage of Selby-bound cargoes.

James W Cook & Company's tanker barge *Lapwing C,* built at Dunstons in 1948, enters Whitley lock in 1968 loaded with petrol for Leeds. *Norman Burnitt*

This 1900s postcard view features the rare sight of a keel under sail on the A&CN as it leaves the smaller of Whitley locks with a steam tug and barges waiting to use the larger lock.

The smaller one of Whitley locks had been closed for many years and converted for pleasure craft moorings when this picture of Acaster Water Transport's *Freda Carless* was taken as it entered the large lock in September 2000. Acasters bought the 350 ton capacity barge, built at Harkers in 1964, from Flixborough Shipping Company.

With a family background in barge traffic stretching back to the mid-nineteenth century, Wilf Acaster revived their inland waterway activities in 1943 when he started as a carrier delivering mainly sand to glassworks at Leeds, Swinton and Barnsley. Wilf's youngest son Graham joined his father in 1962 and took over the business in 1980 on Wilf's retirement. Graham and his son Karl have since strived in the face of setbacks, such as sudden cancellation of their Goole-York paper traffic, to keep afloat, mainly with deliveries of Trent aggregate to A&C wharves, which they still use their small fleet to make.

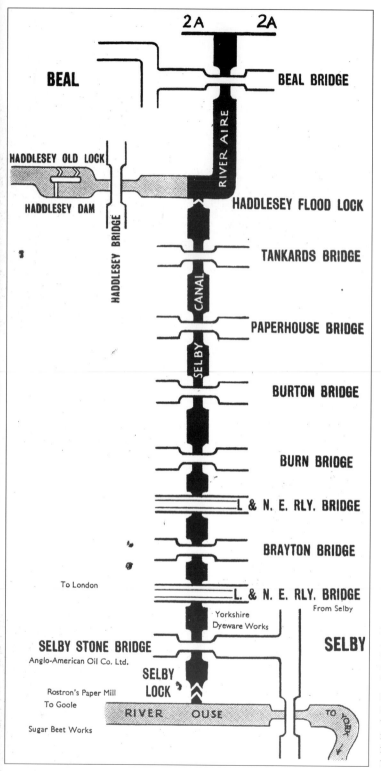

BEAL

2A **2A**

BEAL BRIDGE

RIVER AIRE

HADDLESEY OLD LOCK

HADDLESEY DAM

HADDLESEY BRIDGE

HADDLESEY FLOOD LOCK

CANAL

TANKARDS BRIDGE

SELBY

PAPERHOUSE BRIDGE

BURTON BRIDGE

BURN BRIDGE

L & N. E. RLY. BRIDGE

BRAYTON BRIDGE

To London

L & N. E. RLY. BRIDGE

From Selby

Yorkshire
Dyeware Works

SELBY STONE BRIDGE

SELBY

Anglo-American Oil Co. Ltd.

**SELBY
LOCK**

Rostron's Paper Mill
To Goole

RIVER OUSE

TO YORK

Sugar Beet Works

After joining the River Aire below Bank Dole lock, craft continue downriver for six miles before reaching Haddlesey flood lock at the entrance to the Selby Canal which leads to the River Ouse five and a half miles away. The Selby Canal was opened in 1778 and immediately offered a more convenient route to the Ouse than the shoal-littered and tidal lower Aire accessed through Haddlesey river lock (eventually closed in the 1930s). By 1780, the A&CNC had closed their offices at Airmyn and transhipment to/from sea-going vessels then took place at Selby.

In 1783, nine 70-ton capacity sloops were built by the A&CNC for a Selby-Hull service, augmented in 1795 by a further twenty-three new vessels which were horse-hauled between Leeds and Selby and sailed on the Selby-Hull tidal waters. In 1821, a flyboat service was introduced from Leeds and Wakefield to Selby using four craft built at Lake Lock yard. With about four fifths of all A&C traffic passing via Selby and traffic increasing as cross-Pennine routes were opened, the Selby Canal became very congested. This eventually led to construction of the Knottingley & Goole Canal, opened in 1826, which saw Selby lose most of the canal trade it had enjoyed for forty-eight years. The A&CNC's Selby-Hull services were terminated and the company concentrated on building up a fleet of non-sailing craft to be hauled by steam tugs on their own waterway and by horse on neighbouring waterways. The fleet was twenty-five strong in the 1930s.

Most of the Selby Canal's traffic remaining after 1826, involved additional travel on the River Ouse to/from York. Harkers' 100-ton capacity motor tanker *Victor H* is shown tied up above Burn Bridge on the Selby Canal whilst returning to Yorkshire Tar Distillers at Knottingley with coal tar loaded at York gasworks. *Ron Gosney Collection*

Approaching Selby stone bridge and bound via the River Ouse, for York, the horse hauled wooden barge *Kingfisher* is shown in the 1920s loaded with West Riding coal.

This sea-going sailing vessel facing up the Selby Canal in the 1890s has penned up from the Ouse. On the southern side of the canal opposite the ship's berth, a short arm led off at right-angles to the canal, parallel to the river. Here, cargoes could be transhipped between ships in the river and inland waterway craft on the arm by being lifted over the intervening strip of land without the barges having to leave the canal and enter the often fiercely tidal Ouse.

The motor barge *Daphne* is shown, in this westward-looking view from 1998, repairing bank protection on the lower Aire by placing stone at Hirst Courtney. Across the river from here, 2½ miles below Haddlesey lock lay Weeland, the original eastern extremity of the A&CNC in 1700.

Close to Snaith, two and a half miles further downriver, Alan Oliver's crane barge *Calder* is shown in 2002 loading steel beams brought from Wearside by lorry near a derelict bridge across the Aire. The cargo was then carried upriver to a railway swing-bridge, inaccessible by road, that was to be strengthened.

A loaded sloop under sail obscures a second vessel on this 1890s view of the lower River Aire at Airmyn close to its confluence with the River Ouse. Until 1778, these craft were common here when the village was an important transhipment site. Similar craft were built by the A&CNC in 1783, when the Selby Canal had been opened, to operate a Selby-Hull service. In 1893, Tom Bradley could describe the lower Aire as:

winding through attractive green fields but stinking and much polluted by effluent from vats, sewers and dyehouses at Knottingley and further upstream.

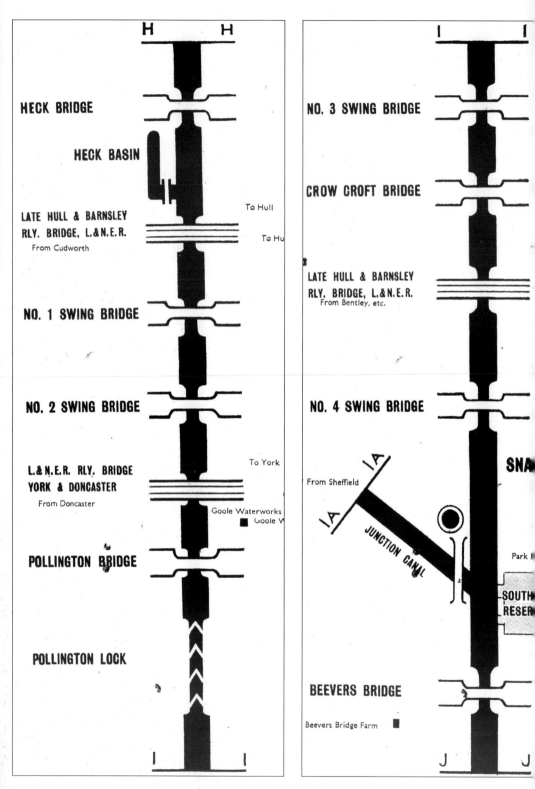

Left panel:

H   H

HECK BRIDGE

HECK BASIN

LATE HULL & BARNSLEY
RLY. BRIDGE, L.&N.E.R.
From Cudworth

To Hull

To Hu

NO. 1 SWING BRIDGE

NO. 2 SWING BRIDGE

L.&N.E.R. RLY. BRIDGE
YORK & DONCASTER
From Doncaster

To York

Goole Waterworks
Goole W

POLLINGTON BRIDGE

POLLINGTON LOCK

I   I

Right panel:

I   I

NO. 3 SWING BRIDGE

CROW CROFT BRIDGE

LATE HULL & BARNSLEY
RLY. BRIDGE, L.&N.E.R.
From Bentley, etc.

NO. 4 SWING BRIDGE

1A   1A

From Sheffield

1A

SNA

JUNCTION CANAL

Park

SOUTH
RESER

BEEVERS BRIDGE

Beevers Bridge Farm

J   J

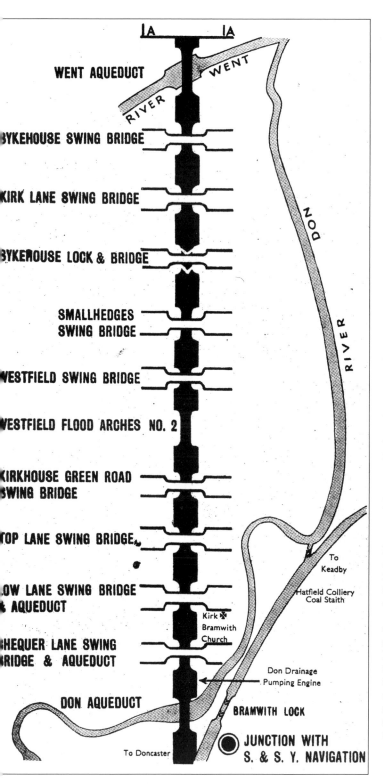

WENT AQUEDUCT

BYKEHOUSE SWING BRIDGE

KIRK LANE SWING BRIDGE

BYKEHOUSE LOCK & BRIDGE

SMALLHEDGES
SWING BRIDGE

WESTFIELD SWING BRIDGE

WESTFIELD FLOOD ARCHES NO. 2

KIRKHOUSE GREEN ROAD
SWING BRIDGE

TOP LANE SWING BRIDGE

LOW LANE SWING BRIDGE
& AQUEDUCT

CHEQUER LANE SWING
BRIDGE & AQUEDUCT

DON AQUEDUCT

To Doncaster

RIVER WENT

DON

RIVER

To Keadby

Hatfield Colliery Coal Staith

Kirk Bramwith Church

Don Drainage Pumping Engine

BRAMWITH LOCK

JUNCTION WITH
S. & S. Y. NAVIGATION

Heck Basin was formerly used to load stone quarried nearby onto craft and the Heck & Wentbridge Railway once came alongside the canal here but commercial activity had declined considerably by the 1930s publication of these strip maps, all of which represent waterways passing through almost flat farmland and small villages. Few cargoes were loaded or discharged at any point on these three maps during the twentieth century with the exception of Heck Basin and a small wharf at Pollington.

Pollington lock, like Whitley large lock and Bulholme lock had dimensions of 483ft x 22ft, throughout most of the twentieth century. The Southfield reservoirs which store water for the navigation and ensure a depth of twenty feet in Goole docks, cover an area of 110 acres and were opened in 1885.

The New Junction Canal, opened in 1905, linked the A&CN with the S&SYN. As built, it was nearly six miles long, dead straight, with one lock, several aqueducts (including major ones over the Don and Went) and nine swing bridges. Bramwith lock on the S&SYN was extended in the early 1930s to allow the puddings to collect coal at Hatfield colliery staithe for delivery to Goole.

When the railway bridge below Heck Basin was being removed in the 1970s, BW hired Waddingtons' motor barge *Rye* to assist. The vessel was filled with water and floated beneath the bridge for a steel framework to be erected as shown. Water was then pumped out of *Rye*, lifting the bridge slightly to enable it to be removed with assistance from a land-based crane. *Joe Batty*

Looking up the navigation from Pollington Bridge, British Waterways' motor barge *Kappa BW*, built by Dunstons in 1954 heads for Knostrop depot in the 1970s. The vessel had been lengthened from its original 76ft to 110ft prior to this photograph being taken, thus increasing its carrying capacity. *BW*

Acasters' *Dumbuck* and Harkers' *Barnsdale H* leave Pollington lock to head up the A&CN in the 1960s. *Dumbuck*, a former AC (ammunition carrying) barge, built as a dumb vessel to be hauled up continental beaches during the First World War, was engined and rebottomed after purchase by Acasters in the 1950s. *V Dickenson*

Like Whitley and Bulholme locks, Pollington lock could accept nineteen-pan pudding trains or merchandise tows of eight barges unbroken for most of the twentieth century with additional conventional craft placed in embayments. This photograph from the 1950s shows a loaded and unbroken pudding train hauled by a steam tug in the lock with another vessel moored alongside. *D&IWE*

With a new lockkeeper's cabin and a gantry over the lock indicating that it is now mechanised, Harkers' *Brocodale H* pens up Pollington Lock in the early 1970s with a cargo of fuel oil for Wakefield.

After a weekend stoppage at Pollington lock, four loaded tankers, including *Cotterdale H*, approach the lock in August 1979 as *Deighton*, loaded with effluent for disposal in the North Sea, and one of Whitakers' modern tankers head down to Goole.

A nineteen-pan pudding train loaded for Goole and hauled by a diesel tug is shown in the 1960s approaching the never-to-be-lifted Hull & Barnsley Railway's Scherzer rolling bridge below Pollington, built in 1884. The A&CN did not become the ship canal it was hoped to be so a lifting mechanism was never fitted. A similar situation existed with the railway swing bridge at Knostrop (page 39). *BW*

Went aqueduct on the New Junction Canal is here under construction in the early 1900s. The A&CN main line is visible to the right of this view. *BW*

Seventeen-pan pudding trains were usual on the New Junction Canal because Sykehouse lock was slightly shorter than those on the A&CN until 1983. The leading unit of the ten-pan rear part of a light pudding train, bound for Doncaster to load smokeless fuel in 1981, is shown being pulled into the lock using lines from the seven-pan, tug and jebus that had already penned up through the lock. Within six years of the date of this photograph, the puddings had finished, BW had sold their freight depots and disposed of their craft. Perhaps as expected, honeyed words to excuse the move again came from those in authority.

Due to its spring-fed and thus purer water supply, the New Junction Canal froze more readily than other A&CN waters. In the severe winter of early 1963, barges head towards Doncaster along a path broken through the ice by a steam pudding tug.

Waddingtons' ex-diesel pudding tug *Allerton Bywater*, here renamed *Strongbow*, pushes the lengthened former dumb barge *No 62* (now *Resilience*) towards Top Lane lift (formerly swing) bridge and the bridgekeeper's house in 1997. The barge was loaded with fluorspar, imported via Goole, for Rotherham.

The New Junction Canal's Don aqueduct allowed river water to flow into the canal in its earlier days when the river was in flood, as shown on this 1932 photograph, looking north. On the original 1891 plan for the canal, this was shown as a lifting aqueduct. *A West Collection*

During the 1950s, guillotine flood gates were fitted at each end of the Don Aqueduct, to be closed in the event of high river levels and prevent flooding of canalside properties especially at Sykehouse. Branfords' *Cordale* is shown passing beneath the northern gate in 1985, loaded with Trent sand for a Rotherham glassworks.

With Don aqueduct flood gates in the left background, a pudding train loaded at Hatfield staithe and hauled by a diesel tug is shown leaving the S&SYN for the New Junction Canal as it heads for Goole in the 1960s. Chains between pans on the outside of the bending train were loosened at four points to enable this tight turn to be made. Hatfield staithe closed in 1973. *A West Collection*

The motor barge *Jolly Miner* is shown in 1989 leaving the New Junction Canal for the A&CN main line in the vicinity of Southfield reservoirs. The vessel was loaded with limestone for Hull from Cadeby, on the S&SYN above Doncaster.

Steam pudding tug *No 7* pulls empty pans and pushes its jebus towards Beever's Bridge in the 1930s whilst heading up the A&CN. *Humberside Libraries*

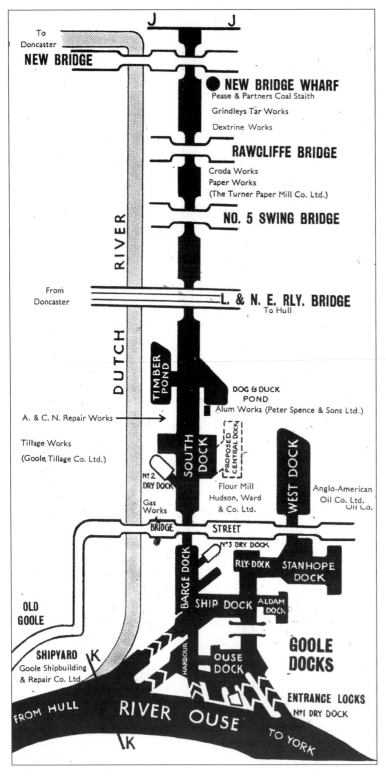

In 1818, John Rennie reported to the A&CNC that the small settlement of Goole was the furthest point up the River Ouse that craft could trade without meeting obstructions from large shoals in the river. Acting on this advice, Goole became the tidal end of the Knottingley & Goole Canal and, quickly replaced Selby as both a transhipment point and direct route to/from Hull for inland waterway craft based in the West Riding.

The Dutch River running close to and parallel with the canal along this length was hastily cut by Vermuyden in 1633 as a flood relief channel to cure problems he had created near Snaith whilst attempting to drain Thorne and Hatfield moors. It was used by craft to reach Thorne Waterside from Goole and, rarely, by vessels wishing to join the S&SYN at Stainforth, until the lock there was closed in 1939.

From 1933, the new coal staithe at New Bridge was served by road from Thorne colliery, a short distance away. In 1939, No 5 swing bridge was replaced by stop gates to seal off the canal from Goole docks in the event of bomb damage to either.

Above the timber pond at Goole, the Waterways Museum and Sobriety Centre are now well-established. The timber pond itself was used to allow wood to season but now supports a boatyard and moorings for pleasure boats.

The A&CNC repair, maintenance and, for a period, boatbuilding yard was opened below the timber pond in 1881.

Branfords' Sheffield size (61½ft x 15½ft) motor barge *Adamant* discharges a cargo to lorry in the early 1970s at a north bank wharf near Rawcliffe Bridge leased from Croda Hydrocarbons. The vessel was purchased by John Branford in the 1960s and crewed by him with his wife, Pat, as mate for several years. *Waterways Museum, Goole*

Rix Petroleum began delivering to A&CN wharves in the late 1990s and here, their *Rix Eagle* passes Croda's premises at Rawcliffe Bridge whilst returning from Castleford after delivering a cargo of oil in 1998.

Rix Petroleum began their inland waterway work on the River Hull at Hull in the mid-1970s after purchase of three Harker tanker barges when that company had ceased carrying. The company has steadily increased its activities since then and is now the major petroleum liquids carrier on the Humber waterways. They built a new 197ft x 20ft tanker *Rix Owl* at Paull shipyard in 2002. *Rix Petroleum*

Just before Easter 1958, steam pudding tug *No 14* came rushing beneath Rawcliffe Bridge much faster than usual. The captain immediately found an explanation for its speed as water gushed through a breach in the bank which separated the canal from the parallel Dutch River. Hoping to get his train of loaded pans to Goole, the captain put on full power but, after five pans had passed the breach, the tow was sucked into the broken bank and actually partially dammed it as shown. The bank was repaired over the Easter holiday and opened for traffic as usual immediately afterwards. *Stan Barrass*

A merchandise tow hauled by an A&CNC tug/barge approaches the railway bridge in the 1900s as it heads out along the canal from Goole towards Wakefield or Leeds. *Brian Masterman Collection*

The bucket dredger *No 3*, one of several introduced by the A&CNC in the mid-nineteenth century, is shown working at the Dog and Duck, Goole in 1935. The dredgings were loaded into shallow-draughted craft and taken out into the Ouse before being shovelled overboard into the river. *A West Collection*

In days of sail, keels and sloops left their mast and sails in the Dog and Duck pond for safe keeping whilst they voyaged inland. Tanker barges trading between the Humber and A&CN wharves in later years often moored here overnight and, in the early 1980s, a diver is preparing to go beneath one of them to remove material thought to be fouling the propellor. His lightweight clothing contrasts markedly with the heavy suit worn by the diver shown on page 41, though only about thirty years separates the two pictures.

GOOLE DOCKS

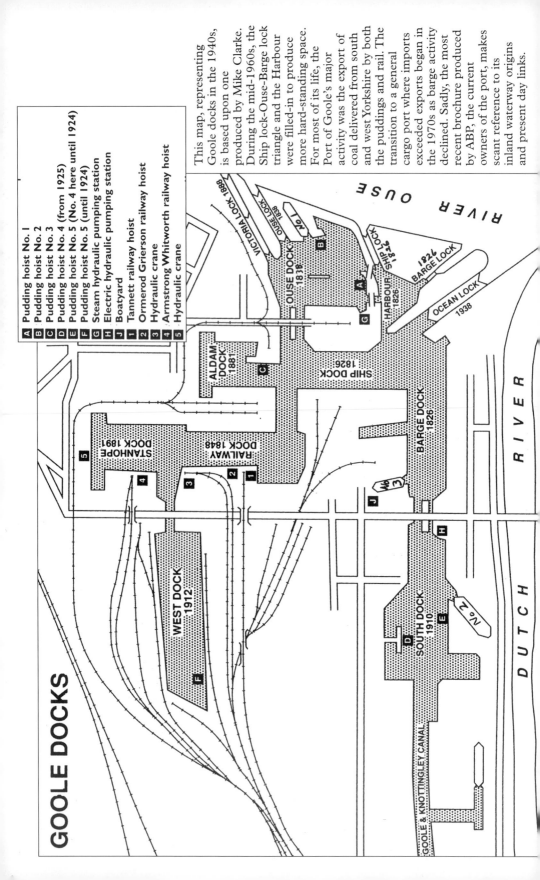

A	Pudding hoist No. 1
B	Pudding hoist No. 2
C	Pudding hoist No. 3
D	Pudding hoist No. 4 (from 1925)
E	Pudding hoist No. 5 (No. 4 here until 1924)
F	Pudding hoist No. 5 (until 1924)
G	Steam hydraulic pumping station
H	Electric hydraulic pumping station
J	Boatyard
1	Tannett railway hoist
2	Ormerod Grierson railway hoist
3	Hydraulic crane
4	Armstrong Whitworth railway hoist
5	Hydraulic crane

This map, representing Goole docks in the 1940s, is based upon one produced by Mike Clarke. During the mid-1960s, the Ship lock-Ouse-Barge lock triangle and the Harbour were filled-in to produce more hard-standing space. For most of its life, the Port of Goole's major activity was the export of coal delivered from south and west Yorkshire by both the puddings and rail. The transition to a general cargo port where imports exceeded exports began in the 1970s as barge activity declined. Sadly, the most recent brochure produced by ABP, the current owners of the port, makes scant reference to its inland waterway origins and present day links.

VICTORIA LOCK 1888

OUSE LOCK 1838

No 1

HARBOUR/SHIP LOCK 1826

BARGE LOCK 1826

OCEAN LOCK 1938

RIVER OUSE

OUSE DOCK 1838

ALDAM DOCK 1881

SHIP DOCK 1826

RAILWAY DOCK 1848

STANHOPE DOCK 1891

BARGE DOCK 1826

No 3

No 2

WEST DOCK 1912

SOUTH DOCK 1910

GOOLE & KNOTTINGLEY CANAL

RIVER

DUTCH

This 1956 aerial view looks west over the port of Goole and shows the A&CN and Dutch River. Victoria Lock, which is undergoing major repairs, and other locations may readily be identified using the foregoing map. *Waterways Museum, Goole*

This advertisement for Camplings dating from the early 1960s, shows *Hatfield*, the one 135hp diesel pudding tug built at their Dog and Duck yard in the late 1950s. Replacement of the steam pudding tugs by diesel craft took place at around this time, with three built by Dunstons and three at E C Jones' yard on the Thames in addition to *Hatfield*.

The Sheffield-size *Sobriety*, is shown on Camplings' Dog and Duck slip in November 1959, marked out for necessary work after a collision and under scrutiny. Acquisition of this vessel began the Sobriety Project, a charitable venture now based in premises across the canal. *Norman Burnitt*

BW's push tug *Freight Pioneer*, built at Goole in 1970, is shown after its naming ceremony on the stretch of water at the rear of the former A&CNC depot. The vessel was designed to operate the ill-fated BACAT system whereby barges were transported across the North Sea to and from Hull by a mother ship to avoid the need for transhipment of cargo at the ports. Hull dockers felt threatened by the scheme and took action to kill it, so it lasted only for about 18 months in the mid-1970s. *BW*

This photograph gives a close-up view of the jebus which was placed immediately behind the tug when it was pulling a loaded train. When not in use with loaded pans, the jebus was pushed in front of the tug.

From the late nineteenth century to the 1950s, the puddings were maintained in the A&CNC's workshops at both Goole and Stanley Ferry, this activity eventually becoming concentrated at the former location. Craft are being riveted and caulked on this photograph from the 1930s.

Puddings are being tipped at No 5 hoist in South Dock into the Bremen-registered coaster *Kambo* as Whitakers' *Battle Stone* passes in 1985, bound for the petroleum jetty t Immingham to reload. The pudding repair shop is visible just beyond the road tankers. Pans were placed onto a hoist's cradle by hydraulic capstans, clamped and then lifted bodily, again hydraulically, before being tipped through 130°. After railways came into Goole docks, hydraulically-powered tipping hoists were also built to tip wagons. At busy times pre-1960, both types of hoists could be found working until midnight, illuminated only by weak paraffin lamps.

Transhipment of imported tar to Whitakers' tanker barges from the coaster *Stella Antares* in South Dock, prior to delivery to Croda's works at Knottingley, is shown on this photograph from 1979.

One of the five pudding hoists used over the years in Goole docks was markedly different from the other four in that it floated by being mounted on a pontoon. It was built in 1908 and is shown in South Dock during 1957, under tow by several steam pudding tugs so that its berth there could be dredged. The floating hoist last worked in 1967 and was subsequently scrapped.

Taken from atop a mill on the north side of South Dock like the picture on page 130, this 1950s view of Barge Dock, Ocean Lock and the Ouse beyond shows a variety of commercial craft, including Cooks' tanker *Woodcock C* heading out towards the A&CN bound for Leeds. *Norman Burnitt*

The pudding tug *No 12* is pictured in 1904 whilst under construction at a yard off Barge Dock adjacent to Bridge Street bridge (labelled 'No 3 Dry Dock' on the strip map on page 122 and 'J' on the sketch map of Goole docks on page 126). *Waterways Museum, Goole*

A view from the 1890s of craft waiting in Barge Dock to be towed up the A&CN by a merchandise tug. Some craft would have been loaded at Goole and others at Hull, to be towed to Goole by one of the Goole & Hull Steam Towing Company's tugs.

B Masterman Collection

This towing ticket would have been given to a by-trader booking to use the general merchandise towing service on the A&CN. The rule, 'heaviest next to the tug' always worried the owner of any well-laden elderly wooden vessel which would subsequently have its timbers flexed constantly for several hours by pulls from both fore and aft. At their peak in the late nineteenth and early twentieth centuries, four or five of these merchandise tows left Goole each working day, bound for wharves up to Leeds or Wakefield.

AIRE AND CALDER NAVIGATION. No. 6954

NOTICE to OWNERS and MASTERS of VESSELS, BOATS or other CRAFT.

Conditions of Towage of Traders' Vessels, Boats or other Craft on the Aire and Calder Navigation.

This Steam Towage Service is provided solely for the purpose of accelerating traffic and in order to obviate the delays and difficulties of horse haulage, the Undertakers of the Aire and Calder Navigation HEREBY GIVE NOTICE that they will only tow Vessels, Boats, or other Craft, by their Steam Tugs, on the following conditions, viz.:—

THAT the Undertakers are not to be answerable or accountable to any person or persons whatever, whether contracting or third parties or any one whatsoever, for any loss whatever (including loss of life) or any damage whatever which may happen to or be occasioned by any Steam Tug or Tugs belonging to the Undertakers, or which may happen to or be occasioned by any person or persons (whether on board the said Tug or Tugs or not) and whether the said Tug or Tugs is or are towing any Vessel, Boat or Craft or not, or for any such loss or damage which may happen to or be occasioned by any Vessel, Boat or Craft (whether such Vessel, Boat or Craft belongs to the Undertakers or not) and whether or not such or any Vessel, Boat or Craft is in Tow of any Steam Tug or Tugs belonging to the Undertakers, or for any such loss or damage which may happen to or be occasioned by any person or persons, property or cargo whatever whether or not on board a Vessel, Boat or Craft (whether in tow as aforesaid or not) and whether belonging to the Undertakers or not) and whether such loss or damage as aforesaid arises from or is occasioned by any breach of any towage contract or any other contract whatever or of any warranty or representation of any kind, or from or by any negligence or default whatever of the Undertakers or their agents or servants or sub-contractors or whether such loss or damage arises from or is occasioned by insufficient towing power or improper use of towing power or any defect or imperfection of any kind whatever in the Steam Tugs or any of them belonging to the Undertakers.

AND THAT the Owner or Owners or other the persons interested in the Vessel or Vessels, Boat or Boats, Craft or Crafts, and/or of the cargo or cargoes on board the same or any of them, which are being towed, or which are the subject of a towing contract with the Undertakers, undertake to bear, satisfy, indemnify and save harmless the Undertakers against all or any such loss or damage as aforesaid (whether suffered by the Undertakers or any one else whatsoever) and against all liability for the same, howsoever such loss or damage as aforesaid arises and howsoever liability for the same is occasioned, and against all costs expenses and charges legal or otherwise in respect of any claims or actions that may arise or be brought against the Undertakers in relation to any such loss or damage as aforesaid whether actual or alleged.

LEEDS, 1st March, 1929.

BY ORDER.

The first pudding hoist for tipping coal into ships was built with a timber frame in 1864 and sited in Ouse Dock as shown on this postcard view from the 1910s. Dumb wooden vessels *Harry*, *George* and *Edward*, forerunners of the Harker tanker fleet, are moored in the left foreground after bringing tar to the port. This hoist was demolished in the 1920s.

The Goole Steam Shipping Company's SS *Humber* is pictured against the eastern wall of Stanhope Dock receiving water and coal bunkers from its owner's barge *West Riding* in 1907. The company's large fleet of ships was responsible for the export of millions of tons of coal brought to the port by rail. The company was sold into railway ownership in 1905, its craft usually then being referred to as 'Railway Boats'. *West Riding*, built at Beverley in 1894, was purchased by the GSSC in 1901 and followed the company through all its changes of ownership until being sold in 1947.

Transfer of cargoes from ship to barge was an extensive activity at Goole and here, a loose cargo of oil seeds is being transhipped to BOCM's *Selby Corrie* in Goole's West Dock in the 1960s for delivery up the Ouse to their mills at Barlby, near Selby.

Waterways Museum, Goole

Loaded petrol tankers and Branfords' *Baysdale* and *Cordale* pen up into Goole docks from the Ouse via the 504ft x 46½ft Victoria Lock in 1984.

Inland waterway craft begin to leave Goole's 1938-built 360ft x 80ft Ocean Lock for the Ouse along with the loaded collier *Perelle* on this 1960 photograph. *Norman Burnitt*

Blow's David, Hunts' Roger and *Evelyn* leave the Ouse, along with several other inland waterway craft, to enter Ocean Lock in the 1950s prior to penning up into Goole docks either to end their voyages here or to continue westwards along the A&CN. *M Guest Collection*

With pudding hoist No 2 and the hydraulic accumulator tower visible in Ouse Dock, the Goole & Hull Steam Towing Company's steam tug *Goole No 4* sets off downriver in the 1930s with a couple of barges in tow, after dropping off the craft it has brought upriver from Hull. Other shipping in mid-river is probably waiting to enter the docks as are the inland waterway craft, with *Serial* partly visible, to the left of the view. The wait at 'tide time' to enter Goole docks via Ocean Lock was often the longest delay of a whole voyage.

Serial was owned by T Fletcher & Sons of Hull. In the 1930s, they brought Finnish woodpulp, imported via Hull, in large vessels to Heath entrance lock where it was transhipped into their smaller craft to be horse-hauled to Barnsley paper mills (page 68). After closure of the Barnsley Canal, the company established a depot at Thornes Lane, Wakefield. Barnsley cargoes were then delivered by lorry from here, as well as grain to Brighouse. In 1969, they acquired Lofthouse basin, near Stanley Ferry and transferred their activities to this site, finishing in 1977. On all their visits to the West Riding, Fletchers' craft loaded a return cargo of coal at Parkhill colliery. *Humberside Libraries*

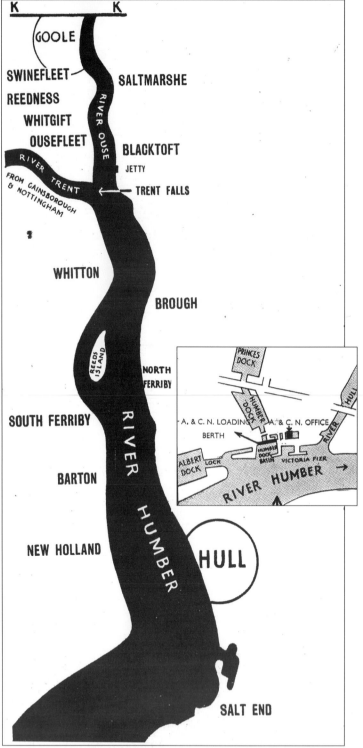

In 1884, the A&CNC became responsible for the Ouse from one mile above Goole, to the confluence of the rivers Trent and Ouse at 'Trent Falls' where the River Humber begins. Blacktoft Jetty had been built in 1874 as a safe mooring for craft unable to complete their voyages on tidal waters to/from Goole on one tide due to fog, adverse winds or shortage of water in the river. It was rebuilt in 1956.

Between 1884 and 1935, the A&CNC spent large amounts of money on construction of training walls on the Ouse. Consequently the channel up to Goole was stabilised and deepened, allowing much larger ships than hitherto to trade to/from the port, as early as the 1890s.

Craft usually came upriver with the tide, leaving Hull about four hours before high water there, and thus used the flow of water to assist their voyages. If possible, they left Goole to come downriver before the tide turned to make similar use of the ebb.

A&CNC vessels often loaded in Humber Dock basin shown on the inset map, though Hull's docks are not all included on this map. In particular Alexandra Dock (opened 1885) and King George Dock (opened 1914), where some craft trading on the A&CN often received or discharged their cargoes, are omitted east of the River Hull.

This map represents a distance of approximately twenty miles compared to some of the strip maps appearing earlier in the book which cover a much shorter distance.

The Goole Steam Shipping Company's SS *Altona* lies on the lower Ouse training wall in August 1908 after trying to avoid a string of barges on the river whilst inward bound from Delfzyl to Goole. The ship floated off almost undamaged on the next tide. To construct the training wall, giant pitch pine piles 40ft long were driven into the edges of the river bed at intervals and blast furnace slag, brought from Teesside in hopper barges, tipped around them.

This 1955 view of the village of Reedness on the south bank of the Ouse, below Goole, was taken at low water and illustrates the extent of bank stoning that had taken place. *ABP*

This postcard view of Blacktoft Jetty dates from the 1910s.

Both sea-going and inland waterway craft used Blacktoft jetty in the 1900s as shown on this postcard view.

Lafarge's ex-tanker *Battle Stone* (see pages 105 and 130) has just left the Ouse for the Humber in 2002 and is preparing to round Apex light and enter the River Trent, bound to load at an aggregate wharf near Newark. Apex light, at the confluence of the two rivers, was built in the 1930s after bank-stoning of both rivers had been completed and was converted to solar power early in the twenty-first century.

A&CNC dumb barges are shown loading cargo for Leeds or Wakefield from horse-hauled drays at Hull's Humber Dock basin in the 1920s. The craft would probably be pulled to Goole by steam tug before joining a merchandise tow from Goole's Barge Dock to their destinations. The A&CNC opened a depot here in 1871. It was closed in the 1980s. *A&CNC*

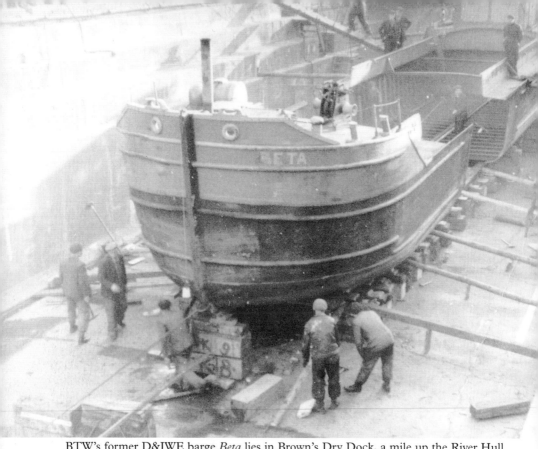

BTW's former D&IWE barge *Beta* lies in Brown's Dry Dock, a mile up the River Hull at Hull in 1956. The 76ft x 15$\frac{1}{2}$ft vessel, built by Harkers at Knottingley in 1949, was being lengthened, a common practice at the time, to 94ft thereby increasing its carrying capacity. The lengthened vessel was shown at work on page 26. *A West Collection*

A&CN craft are loading a bagged cargo (probably raw wool or woodpulp for the manufacture of paper) in Alexandra Dock, Hull, during the 1920s. *A&CNC*

Coal deliveries to Skelton Grange power station, near Leeds (page 43) were halted in Autumn 1974 and here, later that year, Cawoods' barges are being exported from Hull's Alexandra Dock to East Africa aboard the semi-submersible ship *Docklift 2*. Hunts' modern barges followed a similar path shortly after. *ABP*

Harkers' coastal tanker barge *Constance H* is shown on the Humber. During the 1930s and 1940s, the vessel carried many cargoes from both the Stourton and Knottingley depots of Yorkshire Tar Distillers to Billingham-on-Tees. It also traded to King's Lynn, the Thames, Exeter and ports in Belgium and northern France. During the Second World War, the tanker even acted as an escort for two ships at Scapa Flow with one small gun mounted at its stern. *Harkers*

The coastal tanker *Caldergate*, here owned by Esso Petroleum, formerly Anglo-American Oil, was the largest tanker to use the A&CN in the 1930s and, often towing a couple of lighters, delivered many cargoes to the depot in Leeds Tatie Basin. Coming back, as much water ballast had to be loaded to pass under the bridges as petrol that had been taken up the waterway. *Esso Petroleum*

Petroleum liquids for inland waterway destinations were usually collected from Saltend, near Hull, until the 1969 opening of the Associated British Petroleum Terminal on the Humber's south bank at Immingham. This tanker barge traffic was then almost completely transferred to this facility and Whitaker tankers are seen loading cargoes here in 1978.